2

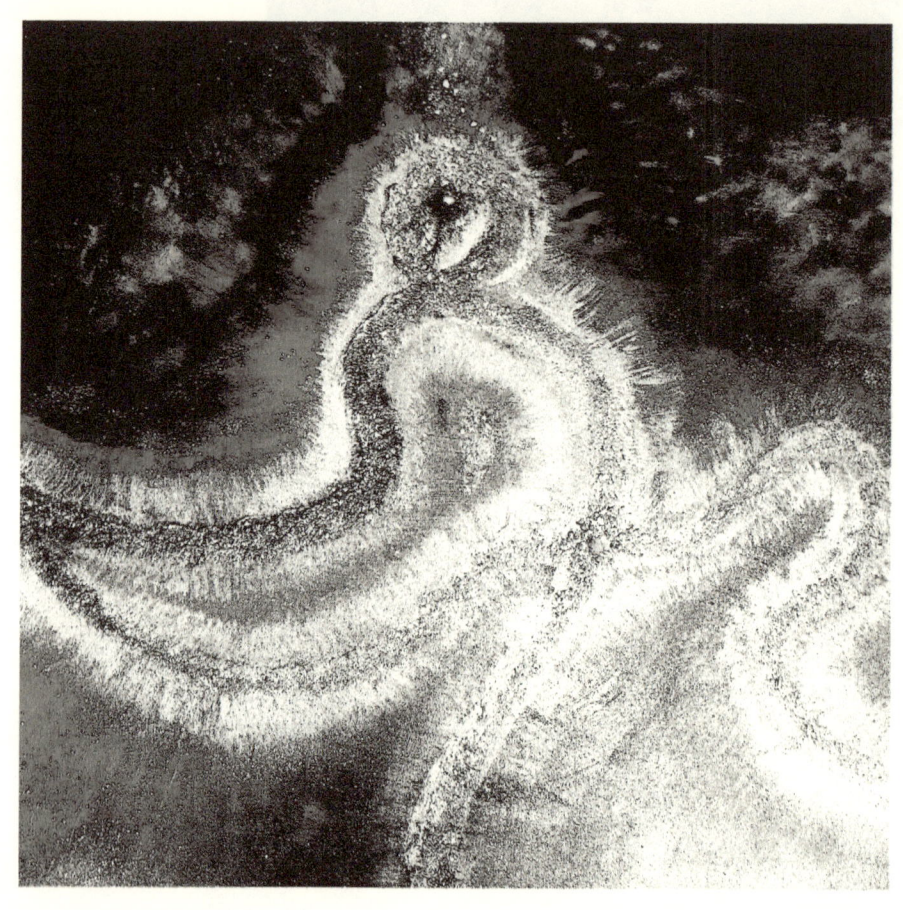

Carl Gustav Jung:

Until you make the unconscious conscious, it will direct your life and you will call it faith.

Quantum Transactional Analysis and New Age

Slowing down, deepening and identifying towards more freedom, autonomy and maturity

By Anne Wuyts

www.annewuyts.be

2016

This book has been published in-house. By printing on demand, there is a temptation to tinker with the content, correct a typo, revise a sentence structure or review the layout. The cover of the book has also been reworked several times. The content of the book is essentially preserved

You are permitted to quote the new concepts (quantum transactional analysis) from this publication and to incorporate them into your own work. You should then mention me. That caresses my ego. In the end I know these concepts were given to me from the Field. They are not my property. This book actually belongs to everyone. That is why I invite you to continue building on my work, just as I build on the works of my predecessors.

Cover: painting acryl on canvas 80 x 80 from Anne Wuyts titled: My being 2012

Word of gratitude

I thank myself because I had the courage to go through my script transforming processes. I took my life back into my own hands. I was a symbiotic and dependent woman. I was a member of a sect. I have paid a lot of money, just to be part of and out of fear to be rejected. I let myself minify and al-lowed the cultists and the guru to speak badly about me. I constantly repeated my dramatic script as a mistreated and abused child. I thought my heavy karma was a punishment and that I had to be a bad person. I was burdened with guilt and had a low self-esteem. I had little self-love, and little self-respect. I mourned for a stillborn child. I had to let go of partners in relationships and I was forced to relocate. I have worked for foolishly greedy bosses in grabbing crazy companies while I craved for recognition. As a true victim I was manipulated and exploited and belittled.

Now, I bow to myself because I successfully went through this painful script transforming mourning processes and I walked my way to an independent, free, mature individuality. The results of what I have experienced and lived through, I share with you in this book.

I also dedicate this book to every individual who has the courage to walk this lonely road in his own way.

<u>I bow</u>

I wish I could bow
In the grass, in the dew
In the park or in the woods
Between the elms
The sun as a witness

I wish I could bow
With open heart and compassion

For the perpetrators
Forgiveness for the mother and the father
The husbands and the traitors

I sing Nafchi Cholat Ahava Techna
Ana Elna Refanala

My heart is wounded
My soul is damaged
My mind is confused
Please Lord
Please heal me

I wish I could bow
The end of victimhood
On my knees
My forehead to the ground
Palms up
And my heart open in sympathy
And love for All that is

I am the perpetrator and the prey
In one and the same
Archetypes that live
In the depths of my shadow
Sometimes it is the perpetrator
Which rudely violates the law
And commits atrocities
And then he dies
And the next time
He returns as the ultimate dupe
Learning from life

I am the perpetrator and the prey
In one and the same
I am the traitor
Living and passing away
In the caves of my shadow
Pulling an pushing
Seeking and hiding
Roaring and howling
Twisting and turning
As a wounded beast

I bow on Holy Saturday
And softly as a human
I embrace my shadow
I fondly welcome the perpetrator
For once he was the pray
I hug and kiss and cradle and marry
My shadow, the chymic wedding

I bow
I no longer am the perpetrator nor the pray
I kneel on the soft moss
Alone in the oakery
The Lord as a witness
Or was it in the green meadow
It is no big deal
My forehead to the ground
My palms to the sky
And my heart open in sympathy
And I only feel love and humility

I bow
There no longer are perpetrators nor preys
The shadow is transposed, composted
Abated, loved and kissed,
Good and evil are transformed
There no longer is betrayal nor sacrifice
Only forgiveness and gratitude

Behold the woman who bows
Alone in the oakery
Birds, Easter flowers, blades of grass
And the sun are witnesses
She kneels on the soft moss
Her forehead against Mother Earth
Who donated her body
Her palms to the sky and the Lord
Who gave a divine soul
With gratitude she puts down her victim cloak

Then she gets up
Behold the old wise woman
Upright and vulnerable
Grey-haired
Which henceforth bears her wounds
With quiet strength and dignity

Content

1. Introduction

"Quantum Transactional Analysis and the New Age" is the sequel to "Quantum Transactional Analysis and Spirituality." This book is a workbook. You are invited to browse on the Internet and additional information can be read in other books. This book also contains references to the first book. It complements and deepens it.

After the introduction you will find a chapter on ego states, script and DISC. Here you will find next to the concept of ego states, concepts such as DISC and social styles. These concepts are compared and the difference is made between working on behavior and working on script. If you work on your script, you let grow your ego states. The evolution of the ego states, in the script transforming process of individuation, towards the integrated Adult is further explored.

Then there is a chapter in which comparisons are made between the Old Age and the New Age, between the old man and the New Man. The New Age people evolve, grow and develop their personality. They are on their way to autonomy, freedom and maturity, their script will be embedded in the script of the quantum era and they participate in creating the New World. They grow to-wards confidence and a high self-esteem. They are free-thinkers who perform phenomenological (self) examination. They know the difference between cause and effect. They learn to see symptoms as the language of the un-conscious and they want to work on the causes that reside in the script. They are proactive and effective and they are in full script transformation towards a winner script. They are characterized by a high intrinsic morality and work every day with the confidence that there is enough for everyone, so they do not need to grab out of fear. In this way, they refuse to participate in the creation of poverty.

In the last chapter we discover the foundations of the New World that is growing slowly and steadily from its basics, while the old world rapidly crumbles. The old world is based on a poverty mind set, power, and faith in science, materialism, capitalism, and immorality. The old world has a self-destructive script and runs down quickly towards poverty, chaos and criminality.

In this book I share my personal perceptions, experiences and what I have lived through. No one has to agree. I want to convince no one. Perhaps this book can inspire you on your quest for answers and it may help you on your way to who you are, always have been and should become again, that it may guide you and accelerate your grow.

2. Script, ego-states and DISC

2.1.Script and script transformation

The life script is like a programming, we have installed as a child, in order to survive in the environment in which we grew up. In our culture lots of people think that children know nothing. That's because the frontal cortex where dwells the analytical deductive thinking is overvalued in our culture. And indeed, this part of the brains must still develop in children. But, make no mistake, children know everything, at their "feeling" brains, the limbic system or mammalian brains and there the script is written. Scripts have a childlike logic and make that we end up again and again in situations that we recognise from the past. So, we are constantly confirmed in our script. If we know that scripts mainly consist of mostly unconscious beliefs about ourselves and the world, and if we know that the things in which we believe often come true, then it is logical that if you transform your beliefs, you create other realities. This is an ultimate form of freedom. And that is the core of quantum transactional analysis.

Of course we get a lot of opportunities in our lives to transform and adapt our script. Subconsciously we do that each time when we are confronted with different frames of reference. We go to school, we learn to read, we read books and we watch television, we visit other people, we graduate, we take a sweetheart, we go to work, we raise a family, we build a house, we promote, we retrain and at the end we retire. Or we live through bad things or traumas such as illness, death, accidents, relationship breakdowns, resignation or bankruptcy. Here we can find opportunities for transformation, but unfortunately, when such disasters occur, people often fall even deeper into their old (losers) script. And that's because we do not know how to grieve.

There are winner scripts and loser scripts. There are dramatic scripts and banal scripts. The good news is that anyone who wants to can transform his script into a winner-script. In your inner journey over here, you discover who you really are, who you essentially have always been and who you can become again. Script transformation is not a pleasant process for transformation happens out of the comfort zone. You leave the familiar frames of reference and discover new frames of reference. That can be a conscious choice or not. If you are forced to leave the familiar frames of reference by for example a restructuring at work, you can do two things, or you can fit your behavioral, and then we speak of 'change', or you can mourn over the old frameworks, building inner strength and seeing the new frames of reference as a challenge to go one step further on your way to greater autonomy and maturity. Here we speak of transformation. Transformation is usually not an agree-able process. The grieving process burns anything that is not essential away. You get closer to the core of who you always were and who you can become again. You develop your own beliefs, your own mind, your own vision and your own mission. That's the individuation process. You become freer, more independent and more mature. In transactional analysis, we call it the Integrated Adult. In book 1, I described in detail this pro-cess. In this book (book 2) I would like to stand still on the matter and to even go deeper into it.

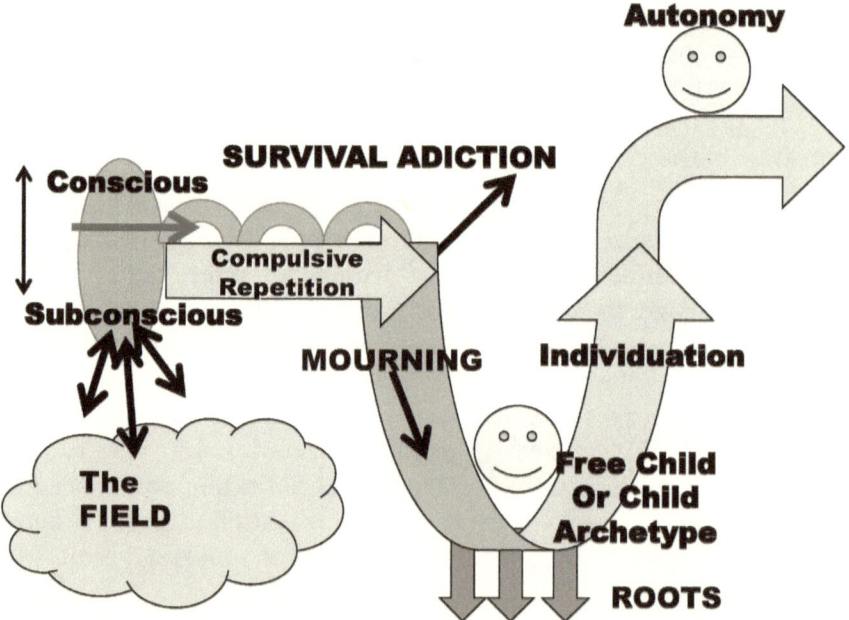

Here you find again (see also book 1) the schema of the transforming process of mourning.

2.2. DISC

If you Google 'DISC' or 'social styles' you get dozens of these diagrams with explanation. There you can read that the DISC tool is a psychometric behavioural test based on the work of William Marston "The Emotions of Normal People". The behaviourist John G. Geier trans-lated these insights into a personality profile. DISC stands for Dominant (red), Influence (yellow), Stable (green) and Conscientiousness (blue).

The DISC model is also related to the model of social behaviour styles, which would be based on the theories of Jung.

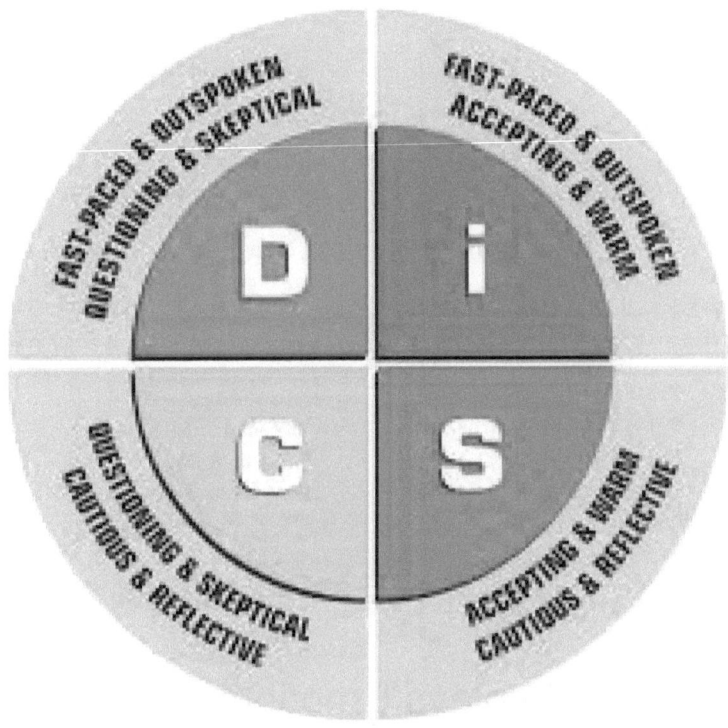

Here we have two interrelated models that are based on observing and analysing human behaviour and that actually tell something about script behaviour. Script behaviour, as opposed to autonomous behaviour is un-free, dependent and immature. It's unconscious behaviour, as it were happening on autopilot. You see your-self acting and speaking, you disagree with what you do or say and how you're doing or saying it and it's like you have no control at all. In the awareness process you ob-serve this behaviour, you're not happy with it, you have the intention to do it differently next time and yet it does not work or it's very difficult. That's because you are working at the behavioural level. Behavioural therapy works only at this level.

Social Styles
David Merrill & Roger Reid

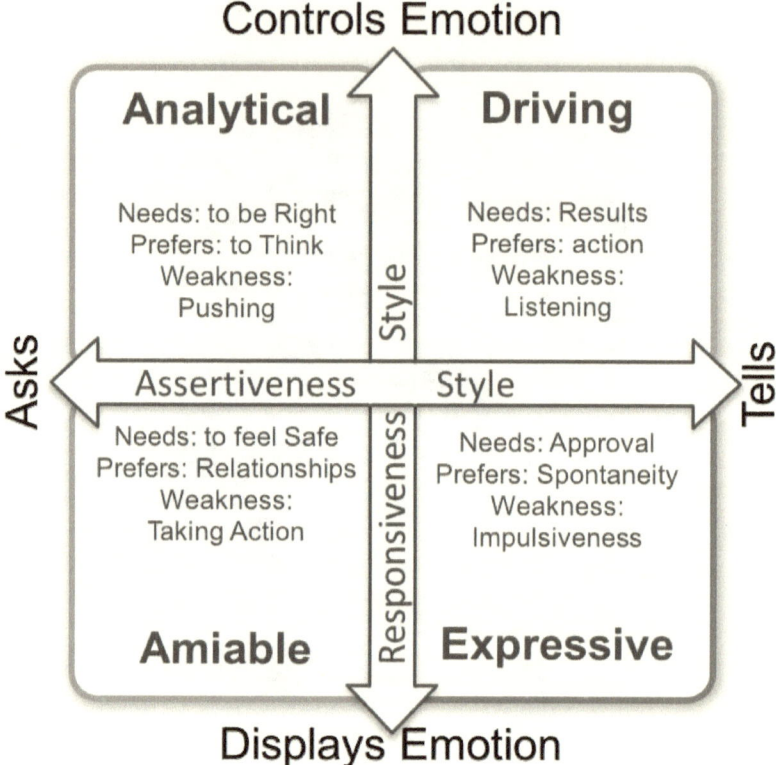

Controls Emotion

Analytical

Needs: to be Right
Prefers: to Think
Weakness:
Pushing

Driving

Needs: Results
Prefers: action
Weakness:
Listening

Asks ← Assertiveness   Style → **Tells**

Style

Amiable

Needs: to feel Safe
Prefers: Relationships
Weakness:
Taking Action

Expressive

Needs: Approval
Prefers: Spontaneity
Weakness:
Impulsiveness

Responsiveness

Displays Emotion

Companies provide attitude trainings using DISC or social behavioural styles to induce more appropriate behaviour. For example,
they want their employees to be more client-oriented, or they
want them to apply the techniques of active listening. And it does
not work. That's because tinkering with behaviour equals tinkering with symptoms. Symptoms are consequences. Tackling the
effect I call change. Tackling the cause, I call transformation and
the causes lie in the deeper layers of the subconscious, which is
the script, which develops in the emotional mammalian brains
from child-hood.

Everyone has a personal script that is embedded in the script of
the bloodline, the family script. Family scripts are embedded in a
cultural script that has grown historically. Thus we can speak of
the Flemish script that we all have a bit of (in Flandres). The more
unconsciously you are, the more you have it. If you transform

your personal script, you transform your family script and also some of the cultural script. Companies also have scripts. Often that script is related to the script of the founder and the cultural script of the country of origin. Within companies, we have the various scripts of the departments. Every-one has experienced how incompatible the seller script is with the production script, or how bad the thinker's script above the glass ceiling communicates with the feeler script on the floor. They are almost two different worlds. When we talk about historical scripts we can look at the script of the different generations. The post-war baby boomers or so-called generation B has a different script than generation X (gen NIX). B as a child experienced no crises. They grew up in the 'golden six-ties'. X has seen parents in fear of dismissal, bankruptcy, and poverty. I experience generation X more as selfish and antisocial. They take care of themselves, go for image and money and they often does not mind if it is at the expense of others. Our current leaders in the economic and political spheres belong to this generation, and I see an asocial and amoral policy of grabbers and profiteers. Indeed, when generation B was in power that happened too, only there was more opposition through demonstrations, strikes and petitions. Generation B has built up social policy. I have the impression that now all will be reduced again. The pampered generation Y got freedom, and had a say in decisions. They were the key children because their mothers also had jobs outdoors. About generation Y much has been written. You can find a lot of information about this generation on the Internet. Only one book has been written about generation X, they actually are called the generation "nix", or a lost generation. About B is little literature. Hippies belong here, and the feminists, two socially engaged and active groups, but more about them in chapter four.

Our own personal script undergoes the influence of the family script, the cultural script and the historical script. So if we transform our own script, we transform a little piece of the larger whole. I'm told that you also transform seven generations before and seven generations after. If so, and many people are busy with script transformation, we can quickly transform the Earth's script, according to the principle of the 100th monkey, or critical mass (see book 1). In my experience a new world begins to develop beside the old world. But there is more to read about this in the last chapter. Back to DISC.

So far, in my experience, I have seen the use of DISC and the social styles only to observe, to analyse and to label. Not as a tool for transformation. Still, it's an interesting model because it is much like the ego states in transactional analysis and it is very similar to the concept of script.

In DISC can be found four behavioural profiles that get a colour each. These profiles are virtually the same as those in the social styles.

Blue represents the analyst. He is also a perfectionist. Red stands for the controller, the director, he is results-oriented and brief. Green represents the facilitator, who is very amiable and helpful. Yellow stands for the promotor. He is expressive and creative. It is important to note that these four behaviour styles are present in each personality structure, however, nearly always different in intensity.

DISC also shows the benefits of each style and what are the challenges. In the attitude training courses, which work with DISC, you are invited to get as much as possible to internalise the positive behaviour of each style. So you learn to manipulate even better. A sales-man learns to recognise the social style of its customers and to mirror it in order to relate more effective so he can gain more customers and sell more. Or a director uses the technique of empathise with the behavioural style of its employees in order to gain their trust so they even work harder for less wage.

2.2.1. Red

The director or controller is independent of what others say or think about him. He is impatient, decisive and goes for the result. In the relationship he's directive, authoritative and imposing. He may seem hard. He is not communicative, gives little explanation and listens bad. He does not shy away from confrontations. He is focused, well organised and goes for a correct execution.

From the view of script analysis we could say at first sight and oversimplified that we are dealing with a traumatised person who verbally or non-verbally had to process the following script messages. I think of the drivers: be strong and hurry up, and the injunctions: do not, do not feel, be no child, have no fun and do not think. You could also say from a transactional analyst's point of view that this person is functioning from an un-evolved normative Parent (positive and negative). Later I will tell how ego states can evolve. In my previous book you'll find a detailed description of this profile on chapter 11: "More light on script transformation".

There you can read about how this profile can develop in a healthy way, how it becomes traumatised and how it can be transformed.

2.2.2. Blue

The analytical perfectionist has the Blue behavioural style. He's thorough, painstakingly and is concerned with details. He closely follows the procedures, or he writes them. He loves structure and is an expert in his field. He is quiet, gathers a lot of information and he is a good listener. He analyses, takes notes, balances, deliberates and cannot decide. He is diplomatic in handling and does not take sides. He agrees if you have a good underpinning argument. He may seem uncertain, be-cause perfectionism often brings with it fear of failure.

Again I see a traumatised person. I am thinking of the driver 'be perfect' and the injunctions 'do not exist, do not, do not feel, be not important, be no child and have no fun'. This person has learned to survive by his Adult ego state and to develop the pseudo-thinking. In my previous book I describe this profile extensively (healthy, traumatised and transformed) also in chapter 11.

2.2.3. Green

Green represents the facilitator or amiable style. These people like to care for others. They want to belong and have a need for harmony, peace and stability. They can relate well, they are empathetic, they can listen and they can give consolation. They are obedient and accommodating. They are sensitive to compliments and they flat-ter easily. They may have a low self-esteem, being not assertive and they like to run with the crowd. They are adapting and not contrarian. In transactional analysis, we see the caring Parent emerge, but also the subjected Child. The healthy, traumatised and transformed version of this profile is also described in my previous book in chapter 11. The driver in the diseased script of this profile is 'please others' the underlying injunction is 'do not exist'.

2.2.4. Yellow

The promoter has in DISC the yellow style. He is an avid optimistic chatty. He knows everybody because he relates easily, although his contacts are superficial. He likes to be the centre of everyone's attention; he knows a lot of jokes and makes others laugh. He is a bad listener. He is creative, dynamic, unpredictable and he can improvise as no other. And yes, here we recognise the

Child ego state, and more specific, the Rebel. He has a "do your best" script, often with a prohibiting on success. More about this profile can be found in my previous book in chapter 11.

These four profiles in most attitude training courses are put down rather caricatured and simplistic. For pure fun, such as playing with Barbie dolls, we can now "dress them up" with a profession, a car, eating habits, travel habits, etc. Here are for pure fun four overdone banter images.

Mr. Green has a caring profession in the service sector. He is a teacher, nurse, kindergarten teacher, elderly helper or counsellor. He drives a MPV, for the kids, grandma and grandpa, the dog and the cat come along on a journey to the campsite somewhere in Spain where they go every year around the same time in order to meet the same people. They also love to come home, where it's comfy. The living room exudes cosiness. There are many flowers and plants. The seat cushions, curtains and wallpaper are assorted. On the dresser are photos of family and friends and the kitchen is decorated with the sayings of the League without a name. Green dresses tastefully with many colours, but not too obvious.

Mr. Yellow works in advertising as a copywriter. He may also be a cartoonist or a stand-up comedian. He likes most to travel with his backpack and his tent seeing where he comes out because he loves adventure. He buys a plane ticket and improvises on the spot, where he meets people he travels further with. He stands out with his clothes, his tattoos, his piercings, his attitude and his car. He falls out of place. He is different from others. His living room is transformed into a studio where he does inventions, or produces artwork.

Mr. Blue is an accountant, physician, math teacher or CFO. He has in his wardrobe six grey trousers, which are all the same, of good quality and comfortable. There also are six ditto blue vests. He has three pairs of black shoes of the same brand. He loves rituals, getting up at the same time, coffee at the same shop at the same hour. He loves routine work. He is addicted to rules and procedures. Because that is safe and it gives much grip. What he does, he does well. When he buys a car it is budgeted. He has all the cars that fit that budget compared and put in an Excel file. The car in the best value for money he buys. He is not tempted by model or colour. His house is cheerless and maintains easily. Voyages are perfectly mapped out in advance. There is certainly no room for adventure or improvisation.

Mr. Red is president, CEO, crisis manager or president. He wears Armani suits and he has a car with charisma, a BMW, a Mercedes or a Tesla. He lives in a villa designed by an interior designer and owns very expensive works of art. He loves solid, antique, rustic, classic or modern. He knows what he wants and he goes for it. When he travels he stays in exclusive resorts or class hotels in exotic places. He takes care of himself, eating healthy and doing sports. His accessories are a beautiful wife and good studying children, which he unfortunately does not see growing up because he is making career.

2.3. Ego states

The three ego states, as Eric Berne observed them, are the Parent, the Adult and the Child.

Personally I think the model of the three ego states being the least static and the closest to reality. Ego states are inner ways of being from which you consciously or unconsciously (script based) can act. The more aware you become, the more autonomy you gain the more you can choose from which ego state you will act and react. Ego states thus evolve as your script transforms. Here's an exposé about ego states being able to evolve and how it happens.

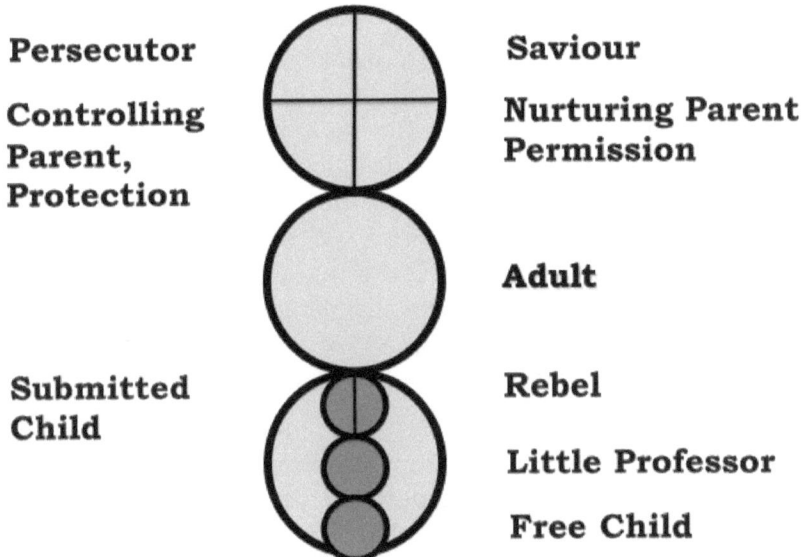

Persecutor

Controlling Parent, Protection

Submitted Child

Saviour

Nurturing Parent Permission

Adult

Rebel

Little Professor

Free Child

2.3.1. The Normative Parent

The positive normative Parent gives structure, standards and assignments. Someone who communicates from the positive normative Parent is guiding and expresses itself often in the directive wise, or the imperative: "Come in, take a seat, sit down, take your book and note." The negative Normative Parent also provides standards but without respect. He induces guilt, accuses, commands and frightens away. His communication style is more aggressive and agitated in the sense of: "Are you finally coming inside instead of standing fiddling there, get in like a lightning, sit on that chair and make notes without squealing!" The red profile often communicates from the normative Parent.

Your inner Normative Parent can evolve by learning to use it in an autonomous way in those situations where it is needed. Laws, standards and structures are desirable because it is safe. Is not it wonderful that everyone drives on the right side of the road and stops at a red light. An undeveloped normative Parent consists of inner parent tapes, which are passed on from generation to generation. These elder tapes consist of habits and rules that you shall not question such as "eat your potatoes!" We observe ourselves sometimes when we just stand there in the same position as our mother or our father and we say the same things as them. We hated them for it, and now we find ourselves doing the same. These are the parent tapes. We observe ourselves acting on autopilot.

With the inner Adult, a very neutral piece in ourselves we can identify these parent tapes, we can observe them, recognise them, question them and decide if they are useful or not. If we feel they are not we can trans-form our script for that matter. I found myself becoming a grandmother at fifty, having a lot of beautiful grandmother tapes, which were nestled in the depths of my script. That was no surprise, because I had two very fostering grandmothers. I could enjoy these grandmother tapes with my grandchild when I baked pancakes for her or when I nurtured her lovingly. Here I observed nurturing elder tapes and there was nothing wrong with them.

Someone with an evolved inner normer has morality and obeys the cosmic law "never do to others what you would not like others to do to you." Standards and structures are given so that we respectfully can interact with each other and they are necessary as long as people are not acting from inner morality. When your actions are based on inner morality your have trans-formed your inner Parent so that it becomes part of the Integrated Adult. Berne calls this Ethos.

2.3.2. The Nurturing Parent

The positive nurturing Parent gives authorisations. The caring Parent communicates in a permissive way: "You may come in, it's okay to take that chair and to sit down, you may take your book and write the next one." The inner Parent is an educator, a leader and a facilitator. It is good to give freedom within structures. The nurturing Parent cooperates with the normative Parent. Managers can give permission to, for example, work at home, or to come to work and to go home at times you choose. In the end, you have to prove that you have worked 37 hours, you've handled your files or you have completed your assignments. This practice requires a certain degree of maturity of both the executive who has to be confident and the employee who has to take responsibility. Fortunately we can see it happening more and more. The nurturing Parent supports, facilitates, encourages and strokes (giving compliments). You could argue that people, who fulfil Parent functions such as parents, teachers, leaders, police officers, and controllers of all types, can invite people to grow by making use of the normative and the nurturing Parent. The concept of situational leadership by Hersey and Blanchard is based on that principle.

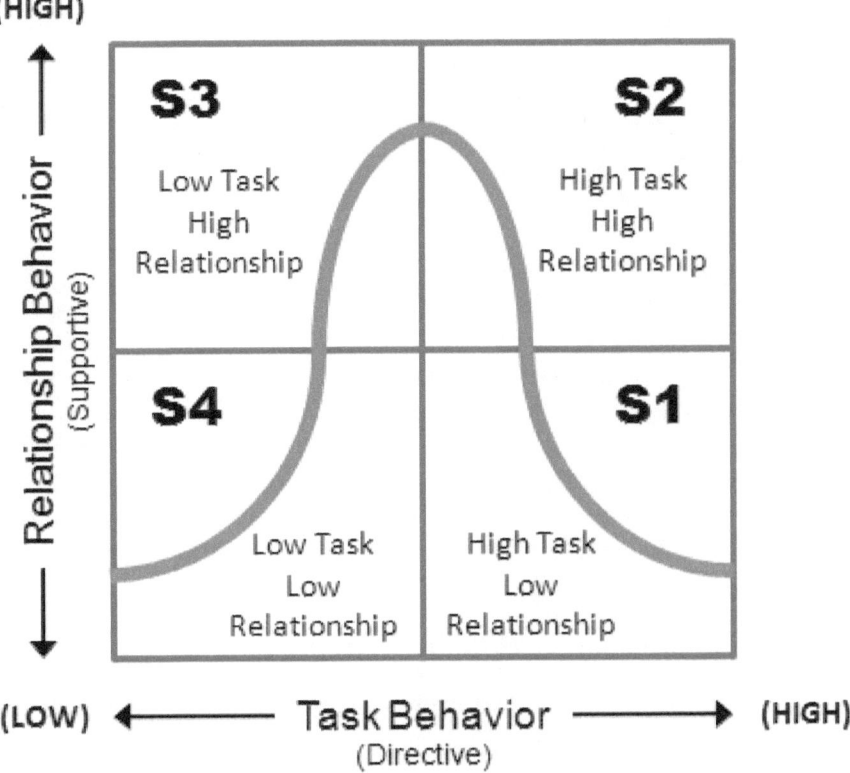

On Google again, you can find a lot of these models with corresponding explanations. Style 1 stands for a lot of direction and little support. It is the directive style. The normative Parent teaches the employee who is highly motivated, but with little task maturity, his job. Style 2 appeals to both the normative and the caring Parent. The employee who gets his job under control, but is often insecure, receives a lot of direction and a lot of sup-port. Style 3 relies on the caring Parent. The employee is given a lot of freedom to fill in his tasks by himself and the manager encourages him. In style 4 we manage autonomous teams from the Adult. These autonomous teams work independently because the supervisor has brought them at this stage via situational management.

The negative nurturing Parent or Saviour is always busy to take care of everyone and to do good things, without being asked. The Saviour meddles, gives unsolicited advice and imposes. Rescuers and Persecutors keep you small to be big themselves. They do not invite to independency, maturity and freedom, on the contrary. They define because they know what's good for you. The undeveloped nurturing Parent saves in order to have the right to exist. Rescuers have a low self-esteem and little self-love. They save because they yearn for recognition. A developed nurturing Parent supports where necessary, he is empathetic and a good listener. A developed nurturing Parent can let go and let be if there is no request for help. Everyone has the right to grow in his own way and pace and to learn from mistakes, missteps and wrong choices. The transformed parent who is ethical and empathetic is part of Ethos in the integrated in adult.

2.3.3. The Adult

In the diagram on page 20 we find the Adult in the middle sphere. The Adult lives in the frontal cortex of our brains and is neutral, objective, analytical and deductive. The developed Adult is the freethinker who per-forms phenomenological free inquiry. The evolved Adult does not assume. He is no believer. The evolved Adult knows that in the third dimension, material, physical world there are no truth and no facts. The evolved Adult knows that our reality consists of perceptions, projections, assumptions and interpretations.

Because our reality goes through two filters: the filter of our senses that operate only in the third dimension sensory world and the filter of our assumptions and convictions of the script. What

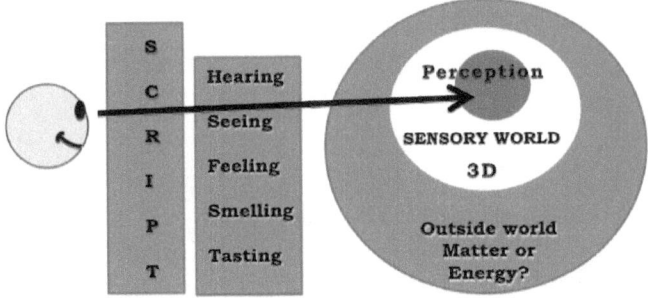

remains are our individual perceptions, projections and interpretations. The evolved Adult, who performs free inquiry in a phenomenological way, knows that. The neutral and evolved Adult considers his own experiences, intuitions and inspirations that he will confront by sharing them. He listens to the experiences and opinions of others by reading about them, to study and to listen to what others are telling and writing. In that way he constantly adjusts his own convictions by broadening and widening his perceptions. Moreover, the evolved Adult goes hand in hand with Ethos (morality and empathy). Berne called the evolved Adult 'Logos'.

The Adult communicates in such way that you are invited to think. The Adult does so by asking questions, especially open questions. The Adult communicates in such a manner that you are invited to make choices, and who makes choices, creates freedom. If we go back to our former example it would sound as: "Are you prepared to come in? How would it be to take a seat? What I propose is that you sit here, is that OK? I think it is a good idea to take your book and to write down the next, does that sounds as a plan?"

The undeveloped Adult is a believer who accepts the al-legations of so-called authorities. For example, the un-developed Adult can believe in science. If it is scientifically proven, he'll take it to be true. He never explored or experienced it. He just believes it. The non-developed Adult believes in dogmas. The undeveloped Adult be-lieves what teachers tell, what reporters present in newspapers or on television, because they should know, should 'not they? The undeveloped Adult believes the pastor, or the Pope, or the imam, or the king or the prime minister, unquestioningly. So, the Adult and the submitted Child go hand in hand.

The undeveloped Adult is able to fully understand a belief, mastering it perfectly and to be an expert in it. Often he imposes his truth as the one and only truth. The undeveloped Adult without inner Parent and thus without empathy and without morality is a psychopath. He is for example able to make an atomic bomb in the belief he is doing well for his country. Either he makes a hydrogen bomb because it is his task and he does so without reflection and without thinking it trough.

Undeveloped believers may indeed believe in the mate-rial objective science. The difference between objective and subjective science is explained in the next section. In my previous book, I went into this matter very deeply.

2.3.4. The Child

Sixty per cent of our energy is located in the inner child. Sometimes people tell: "How is it possible, that this is happening among adults?" Please do not take for granted that we are among adults. Only 15% of our energy lives in the Adult and in addition, many people do not have a developed Adult that also goes for the so-called intellectuals and people that studied among us. They think often materialistic and they often are believers.

In the Child ego state, which resides in the limbic system (mammal brains) houses the unconscious. There the script is written, probably already from conception. Here the emotions dwell: happy, scared, angry and sad. I think the child also resides in the autonomic nervous system, as I have detailed in my previous book. Carl Gustav Jung argued, after he came from India where he examined the concept of karma: "If there is such thing as karma, it is everyone's karma to make the unconscious as much as possible aware." In other words, it's everyone's duty to critically examine his script, his beliefs and his doctrines, which define our behaviour and, if necessary, to transform them. So we create new realities and we free the seven generations before us and the seven next generations. If a lot of people transform their script we may liberate the world's script, which is based on beliefs, lies, manipulation, fear of poverty, greed and selfishness, with all its consequences.

Our script is the cell memory. What's stored in our cells makes us act on autopilot. For many things, we are unconsciously incompetent. That works well until we experience something that makes us realize that we are indeed incapable of doing. Then we become consciously incompetent and we want to become proficient. We can go for it on a behavioural level or at the script level. For example, we find little assertiveness in the Flemish script, except maybe in the generation Y. Mrs Mary Peters concludes that she is not sufficiently assertive, in that way she becomes consciously incompetent. So she decides to follow an assertiveness course and there she learns the technique of DESC. The DESC is a master key that fits in all situations.

DESC

✓ **D** escription of the facts

✓ **E** xpression of emotions

✓ **S** pecification of expectations for the future

✓ **C** onclusion

You can learn it by heart and recite it in a forced way in any situation where you are treated disrespectfully. Now Mrs Peters finds herself in a situation where someone shows no high opinion, remarking in a derogatory way: " Little Marie, once again did not finish her dossiers in time." Several things can happen now:

○ Mrs. Peters freezes and says nothing (script)

○ Mrs. Peters thinks of the DESC she has practiced in assertiveness training and she recites without conviction: "I note that you are accusing me pronouncing my name as a diminutive. I feel not to be taken seriously. I propose for the future we treat each other with respect. If there is something you do not like you can say in a polite manner. I think this would be good for us to cooperate or do you have another suggestion? "

○ But.... her attitude is not congruent with what she says. She looks down and speaks too soft and thus once again she is not taken seriously.

Mrs Peters followed her formation in assertiveness by a training bureau, which provides attitude trainings, and she sees little result concerning her responding consciously incompetent to dis-respect. That's because a lack of assertiveness has a much deeper cause. Mrs Peters is uncertain because she has a low self-esteem, lack of self-worth, lack of self-love and lack of self-respect. The cause of her lack of assertiveness is located in deeper layers of a script where she has learned to survive by adjusting, submitting and saying, "yes" out of fear. In a next assertiveness training Mrs Peters gets a coach who advises her to take some therapy sessi-ons to start working with the causes. And after a while she finds herself suddenly tackling her derogatory colleague in a correct way, she recites the DESC upright and proud with a loud and firm voice. Now she is consciously competent. At this time, the new and desirable behaviour is part of the new, transformed script. Then this new and desirable behaviour becomes a habit and Mrs Peters soon will operate in an unconsciously competent way. You could say that at script level Mrs Peters has transfor-med the drivers "Please others" and "do your best". She has also done something with the injunction 'do not, do not be important and do not growth up.' In this way, when we find ourselves not functioning effectively on autopilot and the desire is there to do some-thing about it, we will, with or without help, little by little transform our script and grow to more autonomy, maturity and freedom. So we develop our Child ego state. If the developed Child is included in the integrated Adult, Berne speaks of Pathos. Pa-thos is part of the integrated Adult as an intelligence, which feels intuitively what is going on. Then the Adult comes for examinati-on and interpretation. Feelings give information, to which you may listen. In my previous book, I talked about the higher self, communicating through the inner child with intuitions and inspi-rations. It is good to listen to your impulses, provided that you are busy with script transformation. Otherwise impulses may ari-se from a dramatic script and lure you in situations that are not desirable. This would not be a disaster either, because these un-wanted situations where you are faced with again and again, can invite you after all to set things in question and to get started with the process of unconsciously incompetent →consciously in-competent →consciously competent→unconsciously competent. In other words, these are invitations to transform your script.

The conflict between the impulses from your script, which resides in the Little Professor or manipulative Child and which invite you to act on autopilot so you get into situations which confirm your script, on the one hand and impulses from your higher self which fall directly into the free Child, and invite you to build on the New World, on the other hand, I call the fourth-degree impasse.

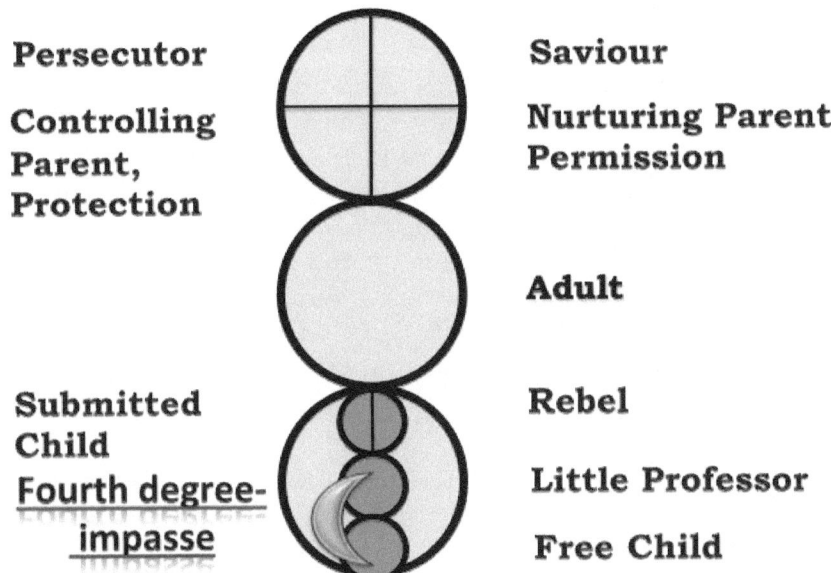

Persecutor	Saviour
Controlling Parent, Protection	Nurturing Parent Permission
	Adult
Submitted Child	Rebel
Fourth degree-impasse	Little Professor
	Free Child

The integrated Adult, as a result of the individuation process in which your ego states have been evolved and transformed, I would like to redefine as follows:

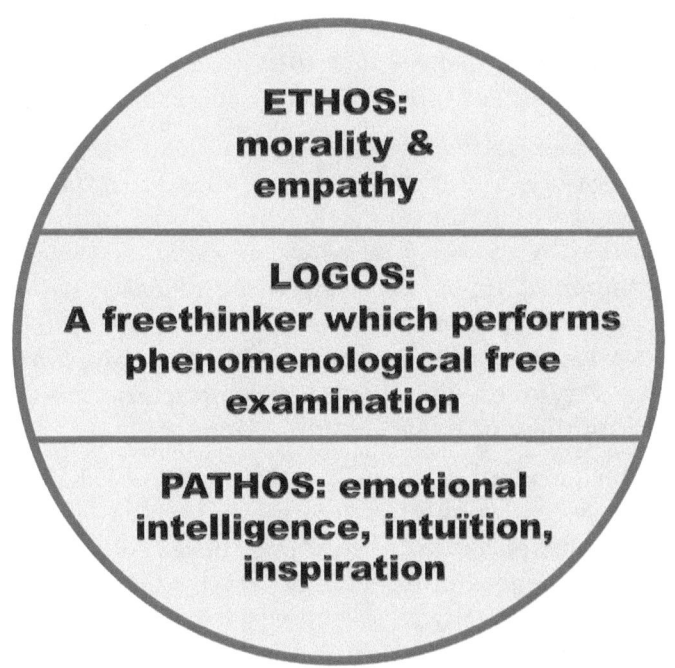

ETHOS: morality & empathy

LOGOS: A freethinker which performs phenomenological free examination

PATHOS: emotional intelligence, intuïtion, inspiration

3. Moral Philosophy & New Age

Here I share some of my definitions, as a result of my new convictions within the new quantum paradigm. It always involves behaviour that we find in the paradigms of the old world, and behaviour that is carried by the transformed script of the new world or new age. In the end you will find a chart so you can decide for yourself where there are still kinks in your (old) script and where you want to go to. You can analyse your personal script, your family script, and the script of the culture in which you live, the historical script in which you grew up and the script of your company or department where you work. More information about effective script transformation you can find in my previous book, "Quantum Transactional Analysis and Spirituality."

3.1. Freethinker or believer

A freethinker knows that we filter reality through the filter of our script beliefs and the filter of our senses. We were born in the third dimension sensory world of Mother Earth and what we detect are projections, interpretations and perceptions. That makes it not easy be-cause there are no facts, no truth and no objectivity in this frame of reference of this new paradigm. Freethinkers who go in search for their truth face difficulties in their free inquiry. Many remain in "I do not believe this" and so they actually indicate they are believers. Or they start to believe in science and so they are also believers. If it is said that it is scientifically proven, they take it and they believe it. Indeed in a world that consists of perceptions it is difficult to do objective scientific research.

Objective or quantitative research means that they try to create clinical laboratory conditions in which the experiments must always be repeated in the same sterile manner with always the same results without the "quality of being" of the researcher being of some influence. In objective scientific research we work with large representative groups investigating drugs and placebos. They work with questionnaires and publish statistics and charts, which then very often can be manipulated at the request and in the interest of the money shooting multinationals.

A freethinker goes out of himself and engages in phenomenological or subjective or qualitative free inquiry. He is his own criterion, and goes out of his own intuitions, inspirations, feelings, experiences, which he shares with others by talking about it, by writing about it, drawing it or express it in other creative ways. He is also receptive to the intuitions, inspirations, feelings and reasoning's of others. He listens, reads, beholds and observes critically for himself and others and is always in search. So he broadens and enlarges his perceptions. By looking at things from different angles and distances. His findings he shares freely, without imposing.

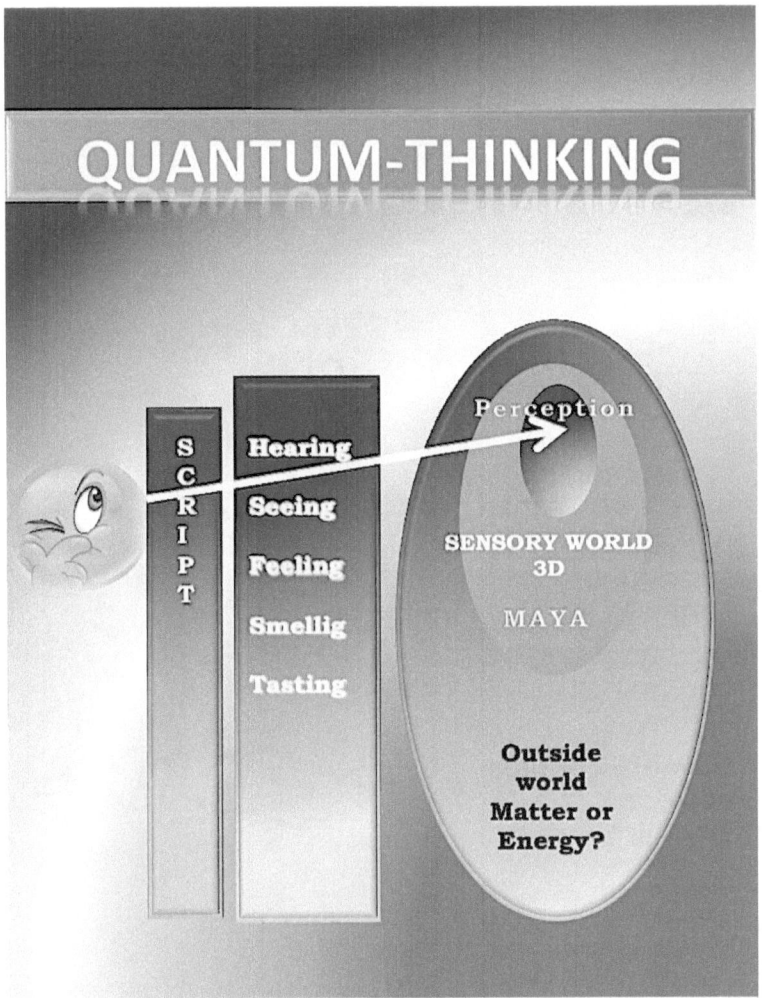

Believers go out of by the church, science, doctors, lawmakers, schools, parents, family, newspapers imposed, taught limited and restrictive frameworks. Often we see that they claim to know what's best for everyone. They tend to impose their truth to others. In Belgium, parents are obliged to have their children vaccinated with polio. Parents, who set up their own schools in order to teach their children to grow to more freedom, autonomy and maturity, still have to follow the imposed programs because their children will be tested on the matter. These programs are stuck in the development stage of integration while the new Age Children need to learn about individuation. Religion remains a required course in our education at school, the alternative is non-confessional ethics, which often preaches disbelief or belief in science. So the indoctrination continues. Believers are willing to use repression and violence and they are prepared to impose by law. Other frames of reference must be rejected in advance without being investigated adequately.

I think our conclusion is logical when we say that conflicts between believers will rather result in violence. For freethinkers will rather communicate, listen and share in order to find a consensus.

Conflict

- If two people have a different perceptions, we speak of a conflict
- How are conflicts between believers?
- How are conflicts between freethinkers?

3.2. Freedom or a noncommittal attitude

It is the desire of every human to be free. However 'freedom' and 'a noncommittal attitude' often are confused. Non-commitment is to do as you wish. Non-commitment is to have it both ways. Non-commitment is to let your life live by others. Non-commitment is refusing to choose and never to go for it.

Freedom, on the contrary, is daring to decide. Freedom is daring to make decisions and to say goodbye to what you do not choose.

Freedom is accepting the consequences of your choices and to learn from the con-sequences. In that sense, there are no good or bad choices. There are choices and decisions. The consequences of your decisions you accept and you learn from it.

Freedom is transforming your script and reviewing your uncon-scious beliefs about yourself and the world. Freedom is doing free phenomenological research, developing your Adult and transfor-ming your script. You build on your own experiences and conclu-sions that you adjust by sharing. Freedom is creating your own reality by transforming your beliefs about yourself and the world. Because that what you are convinced of comes out. That assumes that you transform fear into confidence. A free man is free from addictions and creates his own reality. He takes his life in his hands and he defines his own life pad. That increases his self-image and his self-esteem, which in turn leads to more joy of life and job satisfaction.

3.3. Trust or faith

Faith and trust are often confused. However, for me these terms have a totally different meaning.

Freethinkers, which create freedom, have confidence in themsel-ves and in others. Therefore, they can release the control. They question guarantees and can let them go. They transform fear into confidence and this process they repeat every day. They are their own standard and they are no longer dependent on the opi-nion, the judgment or the approval of others. They trust themsel-ves, they examine freely and they share. They have acquired such because they take themselves, their experiences and what they have lived through seriously. Someone who is in contact with himself relies on the "signals". Experience shows that these syn-chronicities are the language of 'the field'. In confidence the freet-hinker learns to decipher this language, to understand it and to act on it.

Faith is rather based on fear, which perhaps is caused by trauma. Believers tend to put authority outside of them, due to lack of self-confidence. They seek the advice of scientists and professors, or the pastor or an imam. They are going to ask their parents or the family doctor. Believers are not in connection with themselves and rely on the others. They allow themselves to be influenced and manipulated. The others determine their lives, their choices, their decisions, their life path, because they are afraid to choose. If you are out of contact with yourself, as a result of trauma it is difficult to do freely phenomenological research, because the trust in yourself is lost. You trust no longer on your own experiences because you're insecure. Moreover, I find that religions and churches, like insurance companies, banks, and the pharmaceutical industry via the media invoke fear, insecurity, ignorance and guilt to achieve what they want, which is to win as many souls, out of greed and lust for power.

3.4. Spirituality or religion

Bluntly, you could say that autonomous people, freethinkers will tend toward spirituality, because they rely on their own experiences and perceptions. Spirituality becomes an individual experience in which you are in touch with your higher self and the field. Spiritual people rely on their own morality and are guided by their own Ethos. Their bodies and their home are their temple, for which they take care of with love.

Spiritual people are autonomous, they define themselves and they are connected to themselves and their higher self. They do not believe. They experience. They examine and listen to their intuitions that come from their higher self. They are thinkers doing free, phenomenological re-search. Norms and values they possess from them-selves, intrinsic.

They are free and moral beings. Spiritual people live out of gratitude and respect for mother earth, the plants, the animals, the elementals, the people and their cultures, because that's just. They feel that they are part of a larger whole and study what others say or write about it. However, they keep their own standards, testing different frames of reference, without judgment and taking original positions. These views they share with others, without wanting to impose. In my experience, spiritual people, individualities rarely agree on how you experience the 'higher'. It is a unique, intrinsic, individual mystical experience.

Dependent people will tend toward being part of a collectivity, a community, a church or a cult. Others decide what is good or bad and how you should behave. Dependent people, with a tendency to symbiosis will more likely be attracted by a guilt and fear inducing, punishing and rewarding God. A hierarchy-based church guides them. The commandments, norms and values are imposed from the outside. Dependent people submit to the authority of other people. Others define and control their lives. In particular, the church and the church community.

I would like to add that in my experience a lot of unfortunate, traumatised, symbiotically dependent, frightened people go to fortune-tellers and card readers to have their future predicted and to seek comfort in empty promises about love and money. Again, a whole industry is built earning money at the expense of hopelessly disillusioned and depressed people and that too has nothing to do with spirituality. That I call spiritism.

Social workers, coaches and therapists have the task to invite people into their own core strength. The idea is that people who ask for help find themselves quickly back on their own two feet, without them have to walk to a therapist or other professional for years and years.

For me there is still something that has nothing to do with spirituality, but with spiritism. A lot of new-agers think they can create a better world through visualisations and positive thinking. I can assure that some one that never has built up strength through a heavy script transforming mourning process, is not capable to do so. I am invited everywhere to participate in so called world-improving spiritual rituals. And there I only see stupefied believers, lost in wishful thinking contributing nothing at all. In that case, I just spend a nice day in the company of good and kind people.

If you want to be spiritually creative and transformational engaged, you can for instance design your own tarot cards with permissions or you could write a poem or even a book. You could make intuitive paintings. You could design your own clothes and make them. You could decorate your house as a cosy temple where life is good.

3.5. Synchronicity or coincidence

In the old paradigm, with a materialistic world- view, which pretends that the world is made of unrelated substantial building stones, we speak about events that occur and which are of significance, of coincidence.

In the new paradigm, which is based on the quantum field where all is energetically connected to all, we speak with an essential incident that impressed us and stayed with us, of synchronicity (simultaneity).

Carl Gustav Jung introduced the term "synchronicity" as first (1930). He worked with the I Ching. Tarot and astrology can also be explained in this way. You also do not speak of coincidence in constellation work where a group of people comes together, certain topics are covered and these outcomes arise.

If you are going to study synchronicities and you want to learn to understand them, you can see them as a communication tool from the field or your Higher Self, a sign, a language. New Agers sometimes speak of 'serendipity', as in the movie, where two lovers leave it to fate if they will meet again. They are in full confidence.

Working with the field means that you learn to see, de-cipher and understand the synchronicities. If nothing is coincidence, everything has a meaning. What is the meaning of physical symptoms? What does your body tell you with a heart attack? Maybe it means a broken heart? What is it really you cannot digest? Why do you spit bile? What does a dream that's remembered in the morning tells you? What does it mean when you close the front door and you forgot the key? Or how to explain when you miss an important appointment? Coincidence? Or synchronicity? Why do you meet people at certain times and what do they mirror you? What is the meaning of certain events in your life that made you change direction? Or maybe it has a meaning if your car battery is dead, your car does not start, or your brakes do not work? What if your oil tank is empty and you sit in the cold? What if you're burgled and robbed? The sooner you listen to the signals, understand them and act accordingly, the easier you walk on your life path, because the field only reminds you of your prenatal appointments. Often we listen when it is too late and the Field already communicates in capital letters and exclamation marks. We walk with our head against the wall. We have an accident, or we become seriously ill. These are invitations of the field through the messages that are passed as synchronicities to transform our script, to adjust our beliefs, to consciously create our own reality and in that way we are helping in building the New World.

3.6. Transformation or change

Without "change" there can be no transformation. Chan-ge means that you get out of the familiar and intimate comfort zone. If you do that on a voluntarily basis, you find yourself at first in the eustress zone. Eustress is good stress. You accept the challenge. Here you are invited to develop your talents and to adjust to the new situation in a kind way. If you due to circumstances are placed too suddenly and too far out of your comfort zone, we speak of distress: bad stress. Here, the grieving process on the known and familiar situation intensifies. Preferably, the transformation takes place on the border between eustress and distress, by living on the edge. And you can freely choose to, by taking calculated risks. Here, we think, for example, to connect in a relationship with a partner, to take a new job, to build a house, to have children, to travel to a far away land, to go back to school, etc. People who are not willing to grow and obstinately remain in the safe symbiotic comfort zone will often by life itself be thrown in the zone of the distress or even trauma. Think of a restructuring at work, a forced relocation, a loss of a loved one, a serious illness, bankruptcy, being fired etc. Then you need to mourn willingly or unwillingly and to transform, mandatory.

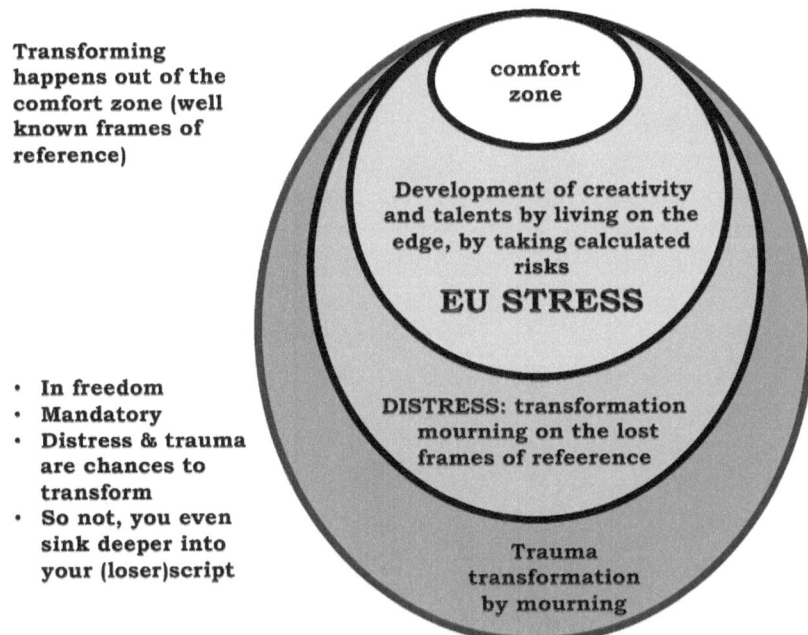

Transforming happens out of the comfort zone (well known frames of reference)

comfort zone

Development of creativity and talents by living on the edge, by taking calculated risks
EU STRESS

- In freedom
- Mandatory
- Distress & trauma are chances to transform
- So not, you even sink deeper into your (loser)script

DISTRESS: transformation mourning on the lost frames of refeerence

Trauma transformation by mourning

There is only one certainty and that is that everything is constantly changing. Most people experience change as something negative. "Change" invites you to step outside the comfort zone where starts the unknown and thus the grieving process on the familiar. The unknown invites anxiety and thus the opportunity to transform. Within the comfort zone, there is no possibility of inner growth towards greater autonomy or freedom or maturity. Creating freedom you do out of the comfort zone, in the area we call "separation". We separate from the comfort zone. Now we're on our own. The grieving process starts. Every grieving process is a transformation process. Provided you don't suppress it with chemical medication. Medication prevents transformation. Home-opathy supports the process.

The question that arises when a change is too large and causes stress is: "And what to do now?" We now have to make choices, make decisions and with every choice we make, we say goodbye to what we do not choose and we create freedom. "Separation" brings disorientation. Disorientation invites you to engage your thinking. Your intelligence must develop. Solutions are being sought. "Thinking outside of the box" is encouraged. New links are being made. Frames of reference are questioned, revised and expanded. You become a free thinker, because believers hold on to limited and restrictive frames of reference. Nothing is the same as before. An identity crisis often follows. Who am I? What am I doing here? What is the meaning of life? You will develop your vision, your mission. Because what you come here to do makes you happy. What makes you happy? You develop a new identity. You get closer to your core of who you really are in reality. Becau-se grieving makes you concise because everything that is not es-sential is questioned and let go. The individuation process starts. An individuality increasingly becomes its own benchmark. Indivi-duals broaden their frames of reference through free thinking. Individuals share their frames of reference, visions, experiences and beliefs with each other. That is the socialization phase. Indi-viduals never impose their beliefs on others. They do not even wish to convince others. They share.

Transforming means becoming more and more who you really are. You do that out of the comfort zone and into the grieving pro-cess. There the individuation pro-cess begins. You develop your freethinking. Your consciousness is growing. Your vibration num-ber increases. Fear is converted to (self-) confidence. Your frame-works are more broadly. You develop your own convictions wit-hout believing. You have experienced it, lived it, and lived it through. You're going to share experiences and convictions, wit-hout imposing. You are ready to connect with yourself and to work with others in autonomous teams or relationships. Change may initiate a transformation process, or not.

Change as such has nothing to do with transformation. You only adjust your behaviour. For, by modifying your behaviour and by submitting, you get positive attention. So you drop deeper and deeper into a comfort zone of mutual symbiotic dependency where you will be asked to copy, to monkey, to reproduce as everyone does. There you are judged on. There you are evaluated on. There you are monitored on. You keep your head under the surface. In this sense "change" induces only status quo. All noses now are in one direction.

Opting for transformation is opting for heart strength, empowerment, responsibility, autonomy, freedom and maturity. Opting for change means choosing for adaptation, dependency, symbiosis and finally (apparent) safety and status quo. In that sense change until now induced no fundamental sustainable improvements. Change makes the burden even greater. Change as such, without any conscious guided transformation process makes individuals, teams, companies and the economy nothing but sicker.

If a company chooses for change, it will tinker with symptoms, as there are structures and peoples behaviour. Employees must follow attitude-training courses in customer service, dealing with aggression and time management. The goal is always to make even more pro-fit at the expense of the working people, to grab more and to fill more pockets. The heart is removed from the company. After a while all falls back into his old business script patterns. Stress diseases, burnout and dis-satisfaction are the result. The vision and the mission wrote out by expensive consultant bureaus, hang some-where on the wall in some conference room and are not taken seriously by any employee. The only winner is the CEO who still gets an extra bonus on top of his ridiculously high wages.

If a company opts for transformation it will for starters express another objective. The mission will be that everyone within the company gets the opportunity to transform his personal script towards more freedom, maturity and autonomy. The company script and the individual section scripts are critically examined. The executives of the upper echelons follow script transformative therapies, and learn to see the behaviour of the people in the departments they manage as a personal mirror. After a while you get genuine independent teams of motivated people who will create added value out of pure pleasure. The manager's walk confidently ahead as an example, and their only purpose is to make them-selves superfluous as quickly as possible.

With great pleasure I red Ricardo Semmler's book, "Semco-style". He describes how in the 90s of the last century he transformed the company of his father into a company that is based on freedom, autonomy and maturity.

3.7. Autonomy or dependency

Autonomous people are independent and free in thinking, feeling and acting. They learn of life. They transform their script in mourning processes belonging to life. So they get closer to their core, because in the grieving process, when you are in the lower depths of hell, anything that is not essential, which is not of the very essence, what does not belong to the core, burns away. Autonomous people are communicating with themselves and are their own standard. Autonomous people are immune to recognition (strokes), approval or disapproval. They are open to feedback. They have taken their lives into their own hands and decide for themselves. Autonomous people are free in the sense that they make choices and decisions. With every choice they make, they create freedom for themselves. Autonomous people are free of survival addictions. Autonomous people are willing to take calculated risks and to step out of the comfort zone (symbiosis). Out of the comfort zone and the familiar frames of reference, they test out the new frames of reference. It's called free examination and freethinking. Freethinkers develop a high moral standard from within themselves. They have respect and love for mother earth, the plants, the animals, the elementals, the people and their cultures.

Dependent, symbiotic people are prepared to be guided by others. They often live in fear and from a survival mode. They are allowing others to determine their lives: family, colleagues, the doctor, the priest, the boss at work... They are willing to sell their souls because they are afraid. They attach themselves in (apparent) safe relationships as a couple, a job, a church or a cult. Symbiotic people do anything to belong and to be accepted by others. They need a lot of recognition and attention from the community in which they live and they adjust their behaviour as such. Dependent people are manipulated and do a lot to achieve status. They attach great importance to ego and image. Dependent people often rely on survival addictions such as smoking, alcohol, drugs, work, games, porn, or anything. They often live from an inner feeling of restlessness and they yearn for heavenly happiness, peace and harmony. They blame the others for the shortage of paradise. They require others for their care and they will care for others from a desire to belong. Dependent people cannot be alone, they need each other and they consider it important what others think of them.

3.8. I or self

The ego is the "little" I that does not develop and that acts out of dependence, fear and a need for power and prestige. Your I need you to get out of symbiosis, go into separation and stand on your own two feet. Thanks to the I you come out of the comfort zone. Out of the symbiosis, you have to walk your way alone for a while. From the little I as the centre you start to feel separate. You experience pain here. This is the grieving process, because your I is vulnerable and sensitive to recognition and betrayal. You have to feel separated from everything and everyone for a while. You are left to your own. Mourning is also dying the little death. That means that your ego dies. You cannot transform without ego. You cannot mourn, or transform, if you feel connected to all there is, from being embedded in a symbiotic way, in the spiritual world. Those who pursue that, I believe, are involved in pseudo-spirituality and do not want to grow. Then you depend on your angels, your guides or "those from above" who will take care of it all for you. That is faith and has nothing to do with trust. Moreover, this way all creativity and entrepreneurial spirit is nipped in the bud. You start living as a monk with a begging hand, depending on your partner, your family, your friends or on social funds.

C.G. Jung makes a distinction between "I" and "self." The "I" is the conscious part of the self. The self consists of the conscious, the personal unconscious and the collective unconscious. The more aware you become, the greater and more differentiated your I becomes. That is what Jung calls the individuation process. It is the task of every person to raise awareness from the unconscious as much as possible. That means that you become aware of your script, that you transform your script, that you recognise and acknowledge your shadow and that you assimilate your shadow, so that you do not start projecting on your outside world. Unfortunately, the I will never become the same as the self. You can strive for it.

Those who individualise get a healthy and high self-image, with self-love, self-respect and self-esteem. The I feels embedded in the larger whole (self) from a transformed script (symbiosis -> separation -> integration -> individuation -> socialisation). He strives for autonomy, individuation and socialisation. Now there is talk of a universal consciousness, Love with a big L. No monkey love. Sometimes that love is hard. That is when you give others the freedom to walk their own path to autonomy in their own way. Everyone has the right to learn from his mistakes. You can let go in confidence. You make yourself subservient, but never at the expense of yourself and you only help if there is an essential request for help. Core power comes from the "I". The unconscious and non-evolved ego is concerned with power and control over others. Pseudo-thinking and acting is from the small, non-developed ego, often with egoistic motives. The I has a quality of being. The I knows from intuition. The I is free and loving. At the moment we are collectively fully in the integration phase, ruled by the ego, which wants to know, to study and to understand. The ego that does not individualise conducts objective scientific research, assumes that things are not energetically connected, disassembles things and tinkers with symptoms.

3.9. Karma or script

"Karma" is a concept that belongs in the spiritual frame of reference. Initially, the concept of "karma" was used in Hinduism and Buddhism. The Theosophists and Rudolf Steiner's anthroposophy reintroduced the concept of "karma" to the west. Your karma is your life's mission. Your karma stands for the lessons you will learn here on earth and what you want to transform. In no way you can see karma as punishment or reward. Good and evil are unknown concepts in the spiritual world. Karma means action and actions have consequences for your-self and others. These consequences you may undergo again, learn from them and transform them. In the spiritual frameworks that talk about reincarnation you can experience the consequences of your actions in your next life. We currently live in a world in full transformation and time is accelerating as we leave the low frequencies of our dense physical matter and evolve to a subtler ethereal dimension, with a higher vibration. In this process, we may experience even faster the consequences of our actions. This happens often in our current life and in my experience even fast after we have performed an action. Karma we create not only with our actions, but also with our intentions. So if we are aware of our intentions and the actions that result from them, we get a grip on the consequences and that is called "working with the Field."

Our script is as it were the materialisation of our karma. In that sense, you are responsible for choosing your parents, the place and time in which you are born and raised and thus of the cultural, historical and familial contexts in which you take your survival decisions and develop your convictions about yourself and the world.

Transforming means that you become aware of your script and that you take responsibility for your actions, your thinking, your feeling and your intentions. By living in confidence on the edge, where you make conscious choices and decisions and where you are willing to learn from the consequences, you transform your script, and your karma. In addition, you create in this way with consciousness, according to the principle of the 100th monkey, freedom in the field. And in doing so, you join in building the New World.

If you are afraid to create karma and you choose not to decide, not to act and not to create, in my opinion you cannot grow. You become a kind of monk begging and meditating. Moreover, if this monk is detached by connecting with anything, he will never be able to grieve in a process of separation. Consequently, he does not give himself the chance to even transform something and I think this is the end of every evolution. This monk longs for the self, being part of the spirit world and has not the courage to de-velop a separate and suffering ego. Of course, it may be that this monk's ego has been trans-formed into the self in past lives. Not for me to judge.

Sometimes I receive a coachee, which I consider as a monk. They are very lovely people who fail to build a life, to build relations-hips and to make money in a creative way. They are unworldly and living in a heavenly dream fantasy. They get nothing off the ground. They behave as victims with a begging hand and they are financially de-pendent on others or society.

3.10. Cause or effect

It is characteristic of our culture that people try to solve problems by tackling the symptoms and by eliminating them. But sympt-oms are consequences. Symptoms are also synchronicities. The unconscious speaks, and if all goes well you listen to them, you take them seriously, you decipher them and you go looking for the causes. Causes are usually nestled into the depths of the childishly written scripts, or in other words in our unconscious beliefs about the world and ourselves. The whole medical industry is based on eliminating in other words suppressing symptoms. In companies they deal with structural changes in order to run the business effectively and efficiently. I see companies with a sick script attracting consultants with ditto sick script. After the re-structuring, employees tell, "the soul of our company is gone." Employees are sent to attitude training courses, where they learned to adapt, in the field of communication or customer service or time management. That is quite a challenge in a company with a customer unfriendly script, where top-down is only sent and not listened, and where the workload is too high to remedy with a course in time management. Families come to the therapist with their problem child who needs urgent treatment, while the family script is dysfunctional and the healthy child responds clearly badly. We want to get rid of the symptom and then just go on the way we were. But this does not work. We do not get the flu from the flu virus. We get the flu because our immune system is weak. And our immune system is weak because we live unhealthy, we eat unhealthy and we work in (emotional) toxic environments. Often we even are not aware of this and we find all that is sickening, even normal, because it is a conviction of our script.

So if we treat symptoms, we are actually combatting the effects. And that leads to nothing. Symptoms only communicate there is a problem on a much deeper level. There is the cause. People get sick, companies create crises, families malfunction because limiting, sick survival beliefs are nested at the basis of the respective scripts. It is because of the limiting beliefs in our shadows that it is going so badly with our health, the economy and the relationships between people. The conclusion is that we have to analyse and remedy at different levels (individual, familial, cultural, historical, businesswise) the limiting beliefs of the respective scripts. Other script beliefs create other realities. The way to a healthier collective life is actually very easy, only the awareness is lacking.

3.11. Male or female power

Female strength is of men and women and the same goes for the masculine strength. Our culture is characterized by an immature male power that exploits and destroys from ego and fear (poverty consciousness). This infantile masculine power creates hierarchical, pyramidal structures. The higher you climb the more power you can abuse. Women usually stop at the "glass ceiling" because they are not interested in that kind of power. Of course there are the usual exceptions and everyone knows a powerful bitch. It is a selfish ego-oriented force, which has nothing to do with power. It is a fear-based controlling force that does not contribute to a "higher good" on the contrary. The communication goes top-down and much is kept secret, withheld or distorted. This creates a double morality, "Listen to my words, but do not look at my deeds." Actions are taken in self-interest, ego and status at the expense of the silent majority. Problems are "solved" with a short-term based mental thinking, which is totally out of connection and which only takes the effects into account (symptoms). It is a "thinking" which is based on meaningless statistics and tables. These apparent solutions create even bigger problems in the long term. Economic crises, poverty and crime are the result. They are the mirrors of our leaders who "govern" from infantile masculine strength, force, ego, selfishness, status, and fear arising from a lack of connection, a lack of intelligence and a lack of morality that are probably the result of underlying traumas.

If people grow into independence and stand in their power, they develop their feminine strength, their core strength, and they invite the masculine strength to also become big. That's difficult. Female power is a patient bed-making and space-creating power. She wears and waits and endures and perseveres. She is connected to all living things and is also connected to the obscure, darkness and death. Female power knows from intuition and receives knowledge and wisdom with her body. Female power is an intelligent, experiencing and sensing force. Feminine power is (self-) confident and knows that everything is okay as it is. Female power flows with the flow, is flexible and pliable. Female power operates from an organic letting happen of what is and what becomes. Democracy and hierarchy are of men. Anarchy and consensus are of women. What men are inclined to mention as chaos from fear of losing themselves, women call freedom and responsibility.

It is the wisdom of the feminine power that creates a bed where the adult producing male power can create, targeted and focused, abstract, analysing, enterprising, truthful, transforming and serving. Many men are happy when they can serve and they gladly serve women. This serving power already brought forth many useful things. Think of your computer, mobile phone, GPS, washing machine, vacuum cleaner ... They make life easier, save time and make room for even more creativity.

3.12 Phenomenological free examination

As I mentioned earlier, in the old Darwinian, Cartesian paradigm scientists perform mainly quantitative or objective research. This is research which searches for general patterns on the basis of a theory or theoretical starting point. One works for example with large, representative groups and control groups receiving a placebo. They try to create laboratory conditions and the investigator should have no effect on the experiment. The experiments should be repeated in the same sterile way and should provide the same results again and again. The aim is to verify the statements, or to falsify them (Karl Popper). They analyse, diagnose, research, measure and disassemble. They use equipment that refines the perception (telescopes, microscopes). Questions lists are filled and poured into statistics or tables. Now everything is proven. The new faith, the new dogma has been installed.

This is called objective scientific research. But ... what is the meaning of "objective" when we know that our perception is filtered twice (the filter of the senses and the filter of the projections?) And besides, what is the role of the researcher? How does the quality of the presence of the investigator affect the study? What is ultimately the value of this so-called quantitative, objective investigation into the third dimension sensory world, where we only deal with perceptions, projections and interpretations?

Phenomenological research or qualitative research is of a totally different order. An autonomous person is his own standard and listens to himself. An autonomous person is in connection with himself. That is, he's in touch with his inner child. Your inner child lives in your cell memory, and in your vegetative system. Your inner child is your sixth sense and gets intuitions and inspirations from your higher self and from the "field". Your inner child is your subconscious. The subconscious is very aware and knows everything from the higher self and the Field. The subconscious is the Field. The sub-conscious is the spiritual world. What we call the conscious is very unconscious. The conscious mind is also limited by your senses and your (script) beliefs. So if you can consciously get in touch with your subconscious, you possess all knowledge, then you can draw off directly from what Steiner calls the Akashic Chronicles. The difficulty is to distinguish what are the pure impulses from your intuitions and the higher self and what are the impulses coming from your script. It is often difficult to disentangle this fourth-degree impasse. I see too many so-called clairvoyants, selling projections and nonsense. Their intuitions and inspirations are not clean because they refuse to transform their script. This is the task of the Adult, the mind. As long as you have not transformed your script, with the help of your Adult, your script pollutes your intuitions. An autonomous, in-dependent and free man trusts his own intuition, trans-forms his script and is developing an integrated Adult.

If you're doing phenomenological research you go out of your own experiences, your own discoveries, your motivations, your thinking, your intuition, your inspirations and your own conclusions. You examine your own frameworks and those of others by reading about it to experience things, to undergo them and to live them through. And if it is correct for you it's OK. It is not the intention that you will impose your results to others, or that you will convince others. You can only share them, regardless of what others think of it. And in sharing we broaden the field of our perceptions and we take back our projections.

3.13. Paradigm

A paradigm is a generally accepted view of the world, which is part of our script. Past people thought that the earth was flat and the sun rotates around the earth. That was the former paradigm. The new paradigm, that the earth is round and circles around the sun, was detested and received with fear and aggression. We are now once again in the transition to another paradigm. The old materialistic, Cartesian, Darwinian paradigm says that everything consists of controllable, measurable matter. The world is made of unconnected building stones and everything and everyone is separated. Our schools, universities, science and religion are based on this paradigm. This "old" paradigm was a necessity in the total transformation of human consciousness here on Earth. Transformation always starts with separation, standing alone, ego, pain and grief.

Humanity went collectively through the phase of feeling separated. Adam and Eve were thrown out of paradise. We also speak of the Gotterdammerung or the Twilight of the Gods, or the five thousand years of Dark Age or the Kali Yuga, were we quietly are coming out. It was the big separation from the symbiotic heavenly. We were ripped apart from the unconsciously being embedded in all embracing. Suddenly we stood naked in the cold. With Enlightenment and the era of science the collective integration phase is introduced. Our schools, universities and science "think" from the old materialistic, Cartesian, Darwinian paradigm where everything is analysed, dissected and dismantled in order to understand and control it. In conventional medicine, we have specialists for the eyes, lungs, stomach .... They do not think in a holistic way and links are not seen.

Last century, the foundation stones were laid for the new quantum paradigm with Albert Einstein, Max Planck, Carl Gustav Jung, Rudolf Steiner, with the discovery of the quantum field of zero point energy alias the collective unconscious, alias the Akashic chronicles. In this paradigm, everything and everyone is connected with each other. Each individual is seen as a co-creator of his present and future reality. Man himself is responsible and there is no room for randomness, powerlessness and victimhood. The world is an integrated system, constantly in motion, a stream of events that mutually influence each other. In that way, the "field" is created and we create our reality consciously or unconsciously in the "field".

This new paradigm is actually very old. In the Far East, one possessed this knowledge for ages, from a symbiotic embedded being in all there is. They had developed a medicine and martial arts on the principles of Ki energy. They did yoga and meditation to unblock the chakras and meridians. The medicine was holistic. They had knowledge of astrology and they built temples and pyramids, which were energetically in contact with certain planets and even galaxies. The science of sacred geometry was applied in all areas of life, medicine, architecture and agriculture.

Collectively, we are in a transition from the stage of integration to the stage of individuation. This period of the new thinking began in the sixties with the hippies and flower power movement. New Age Children are not interested in the knowledge of the integration phase. They will no longer be able to count by heart because they have calculators. The waterways in Belgium? They search them on the Internet, as well as Europe's capitals. They have developed their own SMS language and they do things their own way. New Age Children want to be involved with individuation, with personal development and unfortunately our schools and universities are not ready.

Fortunately, there is an overabundance of spiritual initiatives, workshops, seminars, alternative life schools, gurus, fairs and websites, where searching people are received with open arms and can find what they need. You should certainly be sufficiently developed to distinguish the wheat from the chaff in this new world. But we all did err in our quests for truth, did not we? And we all did learn from our mistakes, did not we?

3.14. Being or doing

Our Western culture is a "do" culture. Doing belongs to our script, because laziness is the devils pillow. We are doing out of habit, out of guilt or from inner confusion. Everyone is active and has increased his activities. By early trauma, most people have a damaged vegetative system, with a constantly restless nervous feeling as a result. That inner restlessness you can appease by "doing": work, hobbies, clubs, voluntary work, sports, activities. Doing, doing, doing, in order not to feel, for feeling brings us into contact with inner dis-order. So we cultivate habits that make us do without having to feel or to be connected. These are the addictions that make us survive. Doing, becomes a flight. Always being on the run as a headless chicken, from here to there. So you're doing well. You gain status and it feeds your ego. You are important because you are busy, busy, busy.

In Eastern cultures one knows more the concept of "being". A Buddha sits under a tree and he simply is. He meditates and let the thoughts flow. Thoughts come and thoughts go as visitors, they are not his. They are guests. This also applies to feelings. He is pure observer, aware, indifferent, without intention and without attention. He looks without seeing, conscious. His eyes directed inwards. He experiences the gaps between the thoughts as blue sky between the clouds, until there is only blue sky, nothingness, emptiness. Now he is one with all there is. He is nothing and he's all. He flows with the flow. He is and he is not and he is one with everything and everyone, connected. Only what is empty can receive. The void is filled, conscious, observing. There is no judgment. There is no good and no bad. Now he is full of energy. He is filled. That energy he shares with dance and song and poetry in his creations. It's called Art. He is an artist, an artist living and celebrating life in his actions, his deeds. His creation is an Art, a Sharing of his quality. Nothing must, no discipline, no habit and no flight. He is pure, creation and sharing.

(From "Tantra the supreme insight" Osho)

In the West we have another task: the individuation process. First, the development of the I, through the ego. Then socialising from the "self." In the West the process of separation and sorrow is fundamental in order to develop your core strength and to start the individuation process. Only then can we learn to Be. What was in the East long ago, naturally, through symbiotic knowing, we need to earn in the West during the integration process. Only then it is truly ours.

3.15. Proactive or reactive

If we study the Belgian script, we have a brilliant example of an old-world script. We observe in many ways a banal "do your best and have no success" script, which floats on a lack of pro-activity, lack of effectiveness, lack of efficiency and in making non-committal unworkable compromises. The problems are approached as they arise. In other words, the symptoms are addressed as they are noticed. If you combat symptoms by thinking just one step ahead, there will occur two or three new problems. It looks like fighting the Hydra-monster. Leaders in many areas, in Belgium take measures that simply bring poverty and stress diseases. The house rents are too high. One monthly salary goes to housing, so single people's life gets very hard. The pensions are too low to pay for care in a nursing home. Old people with a little pension, who do not own their own house, are totally screwed when they loose their partner. Besides, the pension fund is empty, and that everyone knew for decades and decades. No one took action. The symptom is addressed by making people work longer, the result is that talented and well-educated young people find no job. Who works is hounded, two employees do the work of three or one co-worker does the work of two. Of course, overtime is not paid, and the boss puts wages and social security of the staff he did not adopt out of a poverty mind-set in his own pocket. Economics and politics drive on fear of poverty and pursuit of profit. There is grabbing and pockets are filled at the expense of the working population. On the other hand, our leaders throw with money, by reactive and unprofessional policy. When bad things happen, they quickly (reactive) make laws. There is an explosion of new laws and measures. Civil servants cannot keep up. So if a citizen consults an official he is depending on arbitrariness and goodwill. It is not a peculiarity that three officials on the same subject tell three different stories. You are never sure if the obtained information is complete or accurate. Despite the multitude of laws and rules, the lack of norms reigns supreme. Criminals of foreign origin are summoned to leave the country or they just walk around freely because the prisons are full. It should also not be said that the prisons are filled with new Belgians.

Belgium as a result of miscommunication, a refusal to make choices and a reactive script of compromising, has way too many governments. Thus, there is too much double work and there are too many conflicting interests between different decision makers. Belgians are master in improvisation, looking where they come out and then again they improvise. I see our culture deteriorating rapidly and poverty increasing swiftly. Now, measures are taken to save at the expense of sick people. If you are seriously ill, you go bankrupt because of the social funds have long been empty. Older people, who have worked hard all their lives and due to circumstances get without work, are put on a starvation wage, though everyone knows that they will have great difficulty finding a job again.

A proactive policy assumes that you anticipate the problems. You will in time put the highways in order if you know that more cars are coming. You build schools and train teachers if you know that there are more children to come. You invest money in solid pension funds when you know that the population is aging. You provide enough prisons if you take measures that cause in-creased crime. Or better, you take measures that reduce crime. You make laws that go against the high rents and you provide on time social housing. You do not invite foreigners coming from less developed cultures where children do not attend school and girls have to stay at home to do the housework, where illiteracy prevails, where women are oppressed, where gay people are discriminated or even killed. If you allow these people in our culture, you have to educate them so they can adapt. They need to learn our language so that mothers can speak Flemish with their children, so that their children are able to effortlessly follow the lessons in our schools and graduate and contribute. So they do not stay behind what makes them the rest of their lives surviving on social funds. The children of these new Belgians need to be educated in our schools in codes of conduct, in good manners and morality, because you can not expect this of illiterate and oppressed mothers who come from deprived areas and have to raise a dozen children.

3.16. Consensus or compromise

According to the Thomas-Kilmann model - and if you go Googling you'll once again find plenty of pictures as the model below, with explanations - there are different ways to deal with conflicts.

If we apply the concept of script and the concept of ego states from TA on this model, it really gets interesting. Assuming pathological script behaviour, we might say that the negative normative Parent imposes. He communicates from the life position "I'm OK, you're not OK" He inflicts and commands. It is a manager or a parent who wishes others to be obedient and to do what is instructed. It's about someone who thinks he knows what is correct and who controls.

Rescuers admit because they think it gives them the right to exist. The subjected Child always says "yes" out of fear. So it also survives. Rescuers act from the life position "I'm OK, you're not OK". The subjected child acts from "I'm not OK, you're OK."

Dealing with conflicts

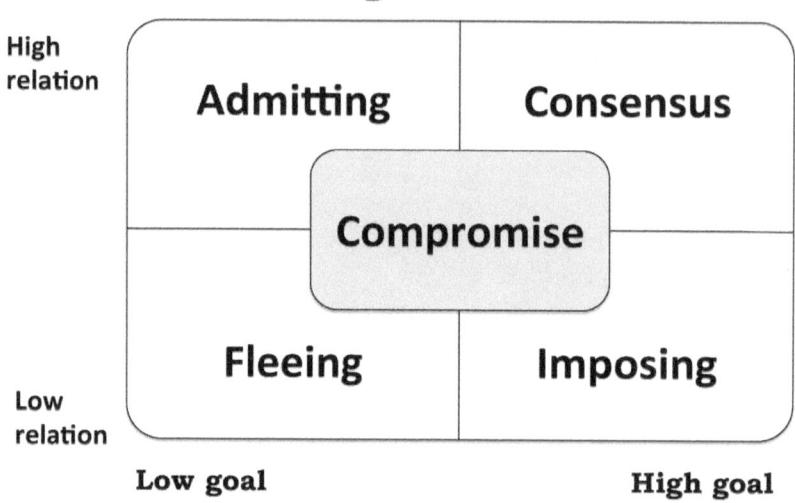

Fleeing means that you run away from the conflict, you avoid it, for example by giving your resignation, or by divorcing, or be re-housing. You go out of the way of the conflict. You do not enter into the conflict. This could be the rebel, because he is an expert in separation. You finally leave the familiar frames of reference. You leave the comfort zone because the comfort zone is too hot. You say "no" to the conflict, and you leave. Perhaps the life position here, "I'm OK you're not OK" or maybe "I'm not OK and you're not OK".

The compromise is of the manipulative Child or the Little Professor, the Adult in the Child-ego-state. It is about giving and taking. Two parties who wish to impose are eventually reaching a complicated, unworkable compromise. There is a lack of communication, a lack of willingness to listen, a lack of empathy and a lack of morality. It is about a clash between two scripts, which operate on both sides from "I'm OK, you're not OK". Belgium with all its governments is the result of a mountain of compromises that have been cooked up by our so-called great statesmen. No choices, no decisions are taken, no one is committed, nobody takes responsibility, and no one dares to cut the knots. There is tinkered with symptoms and no one bothered to look at the causes. The result is an unworkable monster on which one is indefinitely tampering and messing. This costs a lot of money and leads only to even more conflicts with even more expensive and more complicated not workable compromises.

The consensus assumes independent, mature and free individualities that are willing to communicate from the Integrated Adult. They are empathetic and ethical and want a solution that is satisfactory to all parties. They take the time to listen to each other and in sharing they come to the conclusion that, in the interest of the bigger picture they have already been agreed, about a lot of things and that the win-win solution was already long for grabs. Confidence and morality are the basis of a consensus.

From the vision of adult, transformed scripts, we can re-examine the other styles. The imposer then becomes the expert who in situations that are urgent and dangerous and that demand for quick decisions and reactions will take the initiative. If a fire breaks out in a building, we're not going to sit down around the table to see what the options are to evacuate the building. We listen to the fireman and do exactly as he says. Or, if all goes well there was already a plan long in advance (proactive) and then we do what the competent persons who were trained for this, instruct us. Here all parties act from the position "I'm OK, you're OK."

Autonomous people can admit when they know they are wrong, or if the objectives are not so important, or because the relationship is at stake. It is a choice and a decision made from the position "I'm OK, you're OK".

From autonomy, freedom and maturity, there is nothing wrong with fleeing. Perhaps you've already done every-thing in your power to resolve the conflict. You communicated with empathy and morality. You've suggested solutions. You've done introspection and looked at your own shadow. You have proposed a mediator. But the other party is not communicative and remains stuck in immaturity, symbiosis, selfishness, unwillingness, imposing and not listening. Well then the decision to leave, to relocate, to resign or to divorce is justified. In transactional analysis, it is good to say goodbye to pathological players. Consciously fleeing can be a way out of the drama triangle.

3.17. The critical mass

In the seventies of the last century scientists were observing a colony of Japanese macaques (monkeys). They wanted to investigate how the hierarchy in this group functioned. They gave the monkeys just not enough sweet boiled potatoes, which they found very tasty, to see how in the hierarchy monkeys dealt with deficit. These potatoes were thrown into the sand. One day a little female ape grabs a sweet potato but her brother wants to take it from her. She runs into the sea and there she discovers she can wash the sand from her potato, which is far tastier. She instructs her siblings how to wash the sweet potatoes in the sea. Quickly a lot of monkeys learn to wash their potatoes in the sea. One day, the critical mass is reached. The umpteenth (100th) monkey is washing its potato in the sea and at that time, all monkeys, including those of the surrounding islands, which were not in contact, wash their food in the sea. This points to the existence of a kind of collective unconsciousness, a kind of group spirit, which operates beyond the individual members of the group. Steiner called this the group soul of a kind. So all animals have a group soul that leads the flock by instinct. And as we just remarked, this group soul can evolve.

Drunvalo Melchizedek, in his book "The geometry of the universe," puts that human development is not linear evolutionary, but gradually, with consciousness jumps, according to the principle of the 100th monkey.

The consciousness quantum leap towards the new paradigm could happen very fast for the entire collective, according to the principle of the 100th monkey. For all who transforms his script transforms pieces of the family script, the cultural script and the historical script. Due to the large influx of foreigners in our region, people which on personality level come from less developed nations get a chance to catch up regarding integration and even individuation. People from symbiotic cultures where women are treated as inferior, enter a culture of equality between men and women. People from a culture where gay people are oppressed, end up in a culture where gay people have enforced tolerance, can marry and adopt children. People from cultures where people are uneducated and illiterate end up in a culture with compulsory school attendance. If within a reasonable time the critical mass skips, everyone will accept the emerging new vision. At that time we collectively enter the gate of the new age. Then the cycle of collective individuation is completed. Then the majority of mankind has an integrated Adult. The majority of humanity will be autonomous, free and mature. Then the Integrated Adult with his inner morality (ethos) triumphs. Then the Child (Pathos) that is wise and listens to inner intuitions will be taken seriously and then free phenomenological research and sharing will be introduced at all levels. Then we get a world where multiculturalism really works enriching and contributes to continuous growth of the greater whole.

3.18. The field

Lynne McTaggart describes in her book: "The field" the story of a group of scientists who accidentally discovered the Zero Point Field, an ocean of microscopic vibrations that connect everything with everything in the universe as a kind of invisible network. At the subatomic level, there is a connection between all matter. We are all part of the field. Actually, we are all one and connected. Zero point energy or free energy is that energy that remains, according to quantum science at absolute zero. This energy fills the entire universe. All matter emerges from a formless energy, also known as free energy. This quantum field contains the DNA structure of the universe. The field is the source of all energy and matter in the universe and is the blueprint of our existence. Scientists discovered that the field is a conscious field and that consciousness itself is an energy field.

Carl Gustav Jung came in his time already to the conclusion of an existence of a collective unconscious, a psychic field that, according to his teaching is shared by all representatives of a race or species. We speak of a kind of group soul.

Rudolf Steiner spoke about the Akashi chronicles. The Hindus who meant by Akashi, a pervasive medium, called ether, or fifth element inspired him. According to Steiner, the Akashi records store all events, thoughts and emotions that have ever taken place on earth.

The principle of the field, we also found in the concept of The Force in Lucas' Star Wars. Chinese people are talking about Chi-energy and Hindus speak of Prana. Probably these are all different faces of the same.

Drunvaldo Melchizedek talks about a kind of energetic grid, which is spread over the earth. All living beings are interconnected via this grid and communicate with each other through this energetic network through their intentions.

We summarise the foregoing in a table, and then we can go on to the final chapter about the new world.

FEATURES OF THE NEW WORLD	FEATURES OF THE OLD WORLD
Autonomy	Dependency & symbiosis
Trust	Belief
Being	Doing to flee
Phenomenological free research from individuation	objective scientific research from integration
"Self" developed from ego	Ego and selfishness
Creating and serving adult male power resting on female power	Infantile, destructive and frightened masculine power
Socialisation & morality	Symbiosis en criminality
Freedom	Non commitment
Quantum Paradigm	Materialism, Cartesianism, Darwinism
Spirituality	Religion
Deciphering synchronicities	believe in coincidence
Transforming script and addressing causes	Acting on autopilot and tinkering with symptoms
Pro-activity	Reactivity
Going for consensus	Making Compromises
Communication from the integrated Adult	Miscommunication & refusing to listen
Creation of wealth	Inducing poverty
Welfare Consciousness	Poverty Consciousness
Building	War and destruction

4. Brave New World

Let me be clear about what I mean by development, an evolved man or a developed society. All features that we find in the left column of the diagram above, for me point to a developed and transformed script. The characteristics on the right side, point to a lack of development. This is about behaviour that takes place on autopilot and is controlled from unconscious and un-evolved ego states. It involves scripts that have not been questioned and rest on parent tapes that were never examined critically.

It is as if the further we go south on our globe, the less evolved cultures we encounter. These are cultures that float on a script of symbiosis and paternalism. Fathers determine the law and women are of no importance. Women and children are seen as a personal possession that serves to maintain the honour of the family. What is meant by honour I rather feel as the ego of men. Families or clans are led by a sort of rigid godfather, chained in traditions, interfering, imposing, deciding for anyone, intimidating and averse to communication and democracy.

Western culture is rather characterised by a script floating on faith in science. The West is experiencing a collective integration to the fullest. In this script, an educated person often is an intellectual, a doctor, or a professor, an academic, a master. He is successful in the sense that he makes a good living, lives in a fancy villa, drives a fancy car, and as accessories has a beautiful wife and good studying children. Such a family then arrives at the therapist with a so-called problem child. Often then it is an intelligent child, that does too short at the status and image of the parents, because it chooses a more creative or artistic direction at school. Maybe it is a New Age Child or Indigo Child that is already in the phase of individuation, much to the aversion of his parents. Here we get within the family a clash between two worlds, the old and the new one. If the New Age Child does not withstand the pressure from the parents it can lose itself in drugs, cutting itself, anorexia or another addiction that is self-destructive. If parents refuse to face their share the so-called problem child can be included in psychiatry, where it has to swallow chemical, suppressing medication.

This clash between two worlds, here in the West occurs also in the classroom at school. Often teachers and especially those of generation X, linger still in the Old World. They are, so to speak of the old school. They find "common knowledge" important and fill

the minds of the students with 'integration' material, such as imposed by programs made by our policy makers also of gen X.
Most children in the class are New Age Children, Indigo Children,
and they do not ask for integration, they want to move forward, to
individuation. They want to learn about transactional analysis
and ego states and script and transforming towards freedom.
They want to receive guidance in order to succeed in the light
work they are bringing. They want to successfully accomplish
their mission in bringing the Earth to a higher dimension.

Now it is true that, when I speak about these issues with adult
trainees in soft skills trainings in companies, many participants
are happy and excited. There, too, I see a great desire to "course
material" that has to do with individuation and personal development. The way in which I interweave these wisdoms in a course
about communication or assertiveness or time management always catches on. From this I conclude that the world, certainly in
our region is ready for the great leap for-ward, namely, from the
old to the new paradigm from collective integration into collective
individuation. On the other hand, I also notice a shadow of resis-
tance. There are always participants that feel shocked and threa-
tened by the new frames of reference I offer and of-ten they manage to convince the higher echelons to bread rob me. That's the
price you pay as a light worker. And that is a challenge to develop
your core strength and to remain confident.

In my previous book, I already indicated that most coachees that
end up in my practice, are stranded light workers who completely
disoriented wander in a spiritual and financial poverty-creating
world, which is full of integration, head knowledge, ego, selfishness, degrees and image. Furthermore this ancient world floats
on a paternalistic, capitalistic economy, where the concept of
"survival of the fittest" is a deeply ingrained belief, which is also
part of the old materialistic Darwinian paradigm. A trainee once
told me she was resigning from a pharmaceutical company where
thirty per cent of the employees were at home with a burnout.
When the HR manager appealed to the board on the matter they
laconically remarked, "here it is the survival of the fittest." If this
is the conviction of a global cultural script, you must not be sur-
prised that thirty per cent of the executives at high economic and
political levels are psychopaths. As previously indicated, a psychopath lacks morality and empathy. He has no inner Parent and
certainly no Ethos. He functions as a predator, purely on his reptilian brains, and he is only concerned with survival at the expense of anything. His frontal cortex, in other words, his Adult is en-

tirely in service of his reptilian brain. He is addicted to exercising control and power. He invites everyone to stay small and preferably also stupid and poor. He is only concerned with profit, exploitation and grabbing. So these so-called aggressive reptiles create a world where chaos, poverty and crime prevail. And in this way these so called reptiles destroy their own old world. By keeping wages low and creating poverty they destroy their own markets.

New people do not thrive in such a system. This makes them searching in a restless and traumatised way to who they are and what they are doing here. Often they have a partner who persistently clings to the old world. They work for a company that is averse to morality and empathy and just chases, exploits and grabs. They come to me desperate, depressive, burned out, stressed, sad and hopeless. All symptoms, that is very familiar to me because once I also struggled them through. They are nice ingredients for a script transforming mourning process towards more freedom, autonomy and maturity.

Recently I see in my practice some so called new Belgians, mostly women, of the Polish, Turkish, Romanian and Moroccan origin. That is interesting regarding the study of 'foreign' scripts and these people often suffer from a very symbiotic and manipulative family script. It is already very particular for women of Moroccan origin to go a therapist, because that is tremendously not done in the Moroccan script. Depressions you solve with prayer, getting married or having babies, and when that does not work, the local imam will perform devil-extruding rituals with mantras from the Koran.

The women of Moroccan origin, who consult me, already are showing exceptional bravery and a high degree of intelligence. They are highly evolved women who are disoriented and who have the courage often behind the backs of their family to enter my consultation room with a request for help. They are depressed and they often see no way out. During all these years I am in contact with the Moroccan script a number of things became clear to me. Here is a caricature of their script. I throw here the Berbers in a heap with the Moroccans, as most Moroccans who arrive here are Berbers. Of course every-one knows the exceptions to this over simplified description of this script. Also in Moroccan culture, you have more and less developed human beings. And every Belgian is acquainted to a developed Moroccan in his office or circle of friends. I describe here the Moroccan script of the ancient world, as it is embedded in Islam. And of course it is only a perception, namely mine.

What I understand from this script is that parents have an important goal, regarding their children, and often they have many children, and that is that children should get married as soon as possible. For in their opinion, marriage makes you happy. Previously, parents intentionally arranged the marriages. From childhood partners were assigned. Daughters were married to the sons of friends or business associates. I have met women who are divorced from such forced marriages, which is certainly not easy. Recently it happens more often, certainly here in the West. We also see that it is normal that young women marry an older man. Women are supposed to serve and younger women adapt easily to an older man. So one day a couple came to me on consultation. He was Turkish in his late forties and she was a twenty-five-year-old Moroccan. They were married out of love, they told me. He had arranged the appointment with me and he came literally to instruct me to tell her she had to be 'sensible'. As I continued asking what he meant, it turned out that he was looking for an ally in an elderly woman to convince his wife to adopt a more obedient and submissive attitude. My response to him was rather disappointing, and I never saw him again. She came back. You could say he was stuck in the undeveloped older tapes that are quite peculiar to its culture, while she felt good in Western culture, where women count. And yes, she sometimes took a quite rebellious and revolting position. Nowadays young people are no longer given in marriage, but the family is doing everything to find a partner. That partner even has not to be "suitable". The pressure to marry is very big and you have to develop certain inner core strength to cope. There was a woman of Moroccan origin who came to see me as her family once again introduced an undeveloped, uneducated and even illegal potential husband. She was over thirty years and her family literally started to panic. She experienced it as very disrespectful that her family was suggesting again and again just anybody as a potential husband. Meanwhile, she is already well into her forties and still single. She now lives alone in an apartment and you do not want to know what the fuss she had to endure, as an unmarried woman living alone is absolutely unacceptable. Only whores do so, and a whore, you are rapidly in this culture. So good sons or daughters get married quickly to please their parents. And parents have accomplished their task if the children are married. So we could say that Muslims do not always marry for love, but out of obedience and gratitude to their parents. Often both partners in this forced constellation feel unhappy. So one day a Flemish woman came to see me for a consult. She was crying in front of my door. She just found out that her great love, a Muslim of Moroccan origin, with whom she was dating for a while and with whom she was very happy, was married behind her back with a young girl from the Rif Mountains, with whom he already had a baby. Some consultations later he came along. I saw a sad, totally tore up young man who did not know what to do. He favoured his mother by marrying a girl of her choice, but he had to give up his dearly loved, a Flemish lady. He was caught between two worlds. He told me literally "I'm trapped." He did not dare to choose for his great love, against the wishes of his mother. Soon he was suffering from severe anxiety attacks, which he finally suppressed by chemical medication, for the devil exorcisms conducted by the imam and organised by his mother did not work. This young Muslim has failed to fully transform his script. His beloved Flemish terminated the relationship. She chose for herself. She wanted to be his wife, not his mistress. She went through a major transforming grieving process.

So we might conclude that in the Moroccan script most marriages are not executed out of love but out of obedience to parents. The parents see it as an act of love for their children as they ensure they marry soon. My conclusion is that in Islam Culture "love" is a rather unknown concept. I see the Muslims who come to see me craving for love. They want a loving relationship with a developed partner in freedom. Few dare to start a relationship with a Westerner. I also know Belgian men who convert to Islam out of love for their wives, so that they are included in her family. For Muslims, it is less a problem if they marry a Western woman, and that also happens.

Now, if we assume that there is no marriage out of love, but out of obedience, then my conclusion is that children are not conceived and born out of love. Maybe these kids are the result of a rape, because how do you call an intercourse without love, taking place out of obedience? I see so often in my Muslim coachees a loveless script, and a great desire for love and affection. Moroccan script I furthermore experience as joyless (have no fun), mindless (do not think) and normless supported by a highly developed "be strong." This symbiotic script is also characterised by a significant lack of autonomy, maturity and freedom.

Then there is something very bad, which characterises the Moroccan script, and that's incest. A lot of Muslims I met in my practice were sexually abused by father, brother, uncle and / or nephew. And not only girls, even boys are sexually abused. Many Moroccans of the second generation - and if Dad marries an illiterate, op-pressed, submissive young woman from the Rif Mountains, they remain stuck for generations in the second generation - are growing up in large families. A dozen siblings is no peculiarity. If you live with so much behind the facade of a single-family home, things has to go wrong. You cannot expect from disadvantaged, oppressed and illiterate mothers, who also do not speak our language and who have to raise a dozen children, giving their children a decent education. As I mentioned earlier in this book, our schools should take responsibility in this matter and our teachers should get a decent training to cope.

I see young children who are left to their fate, in a Western world that is foreign to their parents, or their mother. They have parents who do not lovingly interact with each other and with their children, because they are married and have children of obedience. The house is crowded, no place for yourself and victim to the sexual urges of close relatives. It is quite normal that these trauma-inducing, loveless, joyless and normless contexts lead to identity crises. And the jump from an identity crisis towards extremism, jihadism and criminality is extremely small I should think. I believe it to be no wonder that our prisons are overcrowded with new Belgians. I find it rather amazing that so many new Belgians function well in our society. I see a lot of wisdom and courage in the young Muslim women who, despite the heavy, traumatic childhood they have gone through, still want to go forward, graduate successfully, adapt, work and contribute.

Another shortcoming that characterises Moroccan script is black magic. A Muslim woman told me in confidence that her older brother was killed in an accident caused by black magic. He was happily married to the woman he loved. But that was not to the liking of the woman that was meant for him. She was convinced that the family of this woman had performed dark rituals that made her brother fell down the stairs breaking his neck.

Within this mental and financial poverty inducing and disorienting script that provides so little guidance to children and young people, there is one factor that stands beyond all doubt, and that is their structure giving, very normative, imposing religion, Islam.

In my experience the Catholic script drives on guilt. Islam relies on fear and particularly fear of being possessed by the so-called djinns. In Wikipedia we read, "A djinn is a supernatural invisible creature that according to Islamic traditions which are discussed in the Qur'an, can take possession of people. Men, angels and djinns are according to the Qur'an three life forms with consciousness created by Allah." Furthermore, I know from a reliable source (my clients) that humans are made of clay, the angels of light and the djinns from fire. You can prevent to be possessed by living devoutly, by purifying yourself in ritual purifications and by sticking to the so-called five pillars of Islam. You have to believe that there is only one god, Allah, and Muhammad is his prophet. You have to pray five times a day faced to Mecca. You have to eat halal food and you must fast at Ramadan. You cannot eat pork. Beggars you should give alms and once in your life you make a pilgrimage to Mecca. These five commandments are already penetrated deep into Western life. Companies provide rooms for prayer, in Ramadan we expect Muslims to work less. The Sugar Festival is an official day off and in Moroccan neighbourhoods in Brussels when there is a rummage sale it is no longer allowed to roast pig on the spit.

Muslims are permeated by their religion. Their religion controls their lives in all areas. They feel chosen by their religion and about their religion you can say nothing critical. Assuming the darker side of the Moroccan script as described above to a large extent, we can understand that hate preaching imams easy can abuse this religion, for young people who stay in a severe identity crisis, live in poverty, and feel being the outcasts of the society, will easily be influenced and manipulated towards extremism, jihadism and terrorism. And once again, it is the responsibility of the Belgian authorities with their normless "do your best and have no success" script that does not want to know, that is ineffective, inefficient and responding reactively to symptoms, that sufficient measures against these excesses are not taken for once and for all - and without violence – by addressing the causes. And once again, our schools should do so, by properly trained teachers who not only engage in integration matter. First of all, our teachers should undergo a script transforming individuation process. They should develop a well functioning Parent (Ethos), so that they can lead, guide, facilitate, coach and educate. In other words, in addition to integration they apply individuation and they educate students towards freedom, responsibility, autonomy and maturity. And they must do so, as executives in companies should do, namely by being a living example. We call this "walks your talk." Trainings in transactional analysis, or even in quantum transactional analysis, would be a very good support for these teaching, educating, coaching and managing people. I also strongly suggest to abolish the courses in religion or ethics and to replace them by the course "individuation" or "personality development". This would be two hours far more better spend. All so-called soft skills trainings, which are known in companies – provided they are given in a transforming way and not just for behavioural change - can be given at the level of the pupils. All teachers should undergo these personality-developing trainings so this matter can be integrated into all courses about integration. By the way, not only Muslim children, but all children and especially New Age children or Indigo's would benefit from this kind of education.

As a liberal, humanist therapist you must work carefully and slowly with Muslim coachees. You must examine the script of their culture and their religion with great respect. Meanwhile, I know Muslims who have expanded the framework of their belief structures with concepts such as karma, chakras and chi energy. They consult a homeopath or a micro physiotherapist they perform Kundalini Reiki and they pray while they are in contact in a meditative way with themselves. They make beautiful paintings and they talk about angels in an anthroposophistic sense. You could say that the new world is developing slowly within the symbiotic little evolved loveless, joyless and normless script of the Muslims, even without the life of this beautiful young women at risk. And I admit that at times I do worry. In any case, these Muslims I honour for their courage and their perseverance. They take full part in building the new world. It is not only the greats that bring light and that transform. All small ones, including myself help building.

Above we see a description of how individuals, from all cultures, plodding and stumbling contribute their stone in building the new world. The new world is developing slowly and steadily alongside the old world that is crumbling rapidly. The old world is based on a patriarchal, materialistic, capitalistic, immoral and fearful script, which is propagated by our leaders under the pretext of social political programs while they shamelessly are grabbing and profiteering at the expense of the hard-working citizens. But this script on the basis of the old world appears to be self-defeating. It leads to economic crises that make the rich getting richer and the poor even poorer. We get stock market crashes that lead to world wars. This creates even more poverty in deprived areas, which leads to terrorist attacks, which in turn leads to wars and crises. The United States of America are bankrupt. They went to war too many times. Meanwhile, they are one big bloated bubble of debt. We only have to wait until it bursts. America pauperises and crime only increases. That script of poverty conscious-ness drifts over to Europe. In Belgium, one person in five can barely survive on a financial level.

The salvation does not lie in bringing in Chinese or Canadian or American multinationals, because they belong to the old world and will really not create employment and prosperity. On the contrary, we only bring in immorality and profiteering in this way. In the long run, wages will fall under the threat of departure to low-wage countries. If we go down this road, we will have to make enormous concessions. Charles Dickens is already waiting at the door.

The future lies I think more in encouraging and sup-porting small, individual, creative initiatives. A lot of people do not want to work any longer for a company that chases and grabs and only ever wants more for less. They take unpaid leave to start their own business. But the business premises rents are too high, the charges are too heavy and many go under. A big vacancy of shops in a city is not a good sign.

Now we see the web shops springing up like mushrooms. Via the Internet a whole new world of cheap and quality goods opens. People do not throw things away. Things that are still good, but do not serve us anymore find a second life through the Oxfam fair trade shop or Kapaza or 2ndhand. That increases durability. We see a lot of people start a free secondary occupation. They work for 4/5th for a greedy, ungrateful boss and for the rest they develop their creativity and earn some nice extra cash.

Belgium's SME country and there are business leaders who conduct business with empathy and morality and that are good for their people. They have a healthy mission and a humanitarian vision. They want to contribute to the greater good. In Flanders we certainly have two companies that are known for their spiritual inclination and their philanthropic script: Colruyt and Torfs. It is interesting to read about their values and mission. Personally I find it a bit too symbiotic with family feeling and all, but we're on our way. Triodos Bank, which arose from the anthroposophist movement, also has a mission that belongs in the new world.

Many multinationals, including banks boast with their billions in profits before closing departments and put people on the street. If you act as such your mission is no longer credible. Here we can speak of double morality and immorality, or even better a double immorality.

But never mind the new world has its foundations al-ready stand firm. And I thank and bow to the forerunners who with blood, sweat and tears have put down these foundations. I thank the hippies, a movement that at the late sixties and early seventies of the last century is the born in the United States and more specifi-cally in the campuses California and San Francisco. They brought a message of freedom and peace. They were against the (Vietnam) war with the slogan "make love no war". Later chanted the femi-nists "make love no children" and "boss in own belly." They reac-ted against the prevailing capitalism and materialism. Their be-liefs, often interwoven in their music, the Beatles on head, inspi-red many young people, including myself. They went through life dancing and singing in colourful flowered clothing. We also speak of the flower power move-ment, which reached its peak at the Woodstock Festival. They went living in communes and put the traditional values of the family in question. The shadow of this movement is that they could not always distinguish free-dom and permissiveness, and they feasted on drugs and alcohol. I had coachees who as a child grew up in a commune, and even there we find scripts with many snags.

Around the same time also developed the Black Power movement among African Americans, who strived for equal rights.

And at this time also flourished the feminist movement, or rather the second wave of feminism. The first wave is situated around the turn of the century and the beginning of the last century in England. These were women who wanted to study at colleges, get-ting master's degrees and preferably also wanted to exercise their profession. They were mockingly called "blue stockings". The suf-fragettes, in their struggle for voting rights were more fanatic and not averse from violence. They put the established order on its head by arson attacks. In prisons they went on hunger strike to obtain the status of political prisoner. They saw themselves as soldiers. In the second wave of feminism, the struggles were against domestic and sexual violence, but especially for the right to equal pay for equal work. Lot by feminism inspired psycholo-gists, anthropologists, sociologists and historian wrote interesting books. They among others did on free phenomenological research.

They questioned the patriarchal, paternalistic frameworks and perceptions and offered new insights from a female point of view. We think of Simone De Beauvoir (1908 - 1986), Germaine Greer (1939), Shulamite Firestone (1945-2012), Adrienne Rich (1929-2012), Anja Meulenbelt (1945), Nawal El Saadawi (1931) and many others. History and psychology became suddenly fascinating subjects. The shadow of this movement is that they have invited women into their masculine power. Women went en masse to study and work. In the eighties we experienced economic crises due to an excess supply of graduates baby boomers rushing in upon the job market and, moreover, for the first time women went to work out-doors en masse. The result is that people today earn only half wages and once again men and women are financially dependent on each other, which again significantly curtails freedom.

In the same seventies of the last century grew an ecological awareness and green political parties were born. Environmental movements evolved from the peace movements, which among other things wanted to ban the atomic bomb, the nature conservation and the second wave of the women's liberation. WWF was established in 1961 to protect the species. Greenpeace was born in Canada in 1971. The ecological awareness also brought a new form of agriculture. Rudolf Steiner' biodynamic agriculture came back into force, as all types of organic agriculture and horticulture, which were averse to gene-tic engineering and unhealthy spraying of pesticides and insecticides. New-Agers ate and lived healthy. Organic Food Shops and organic restaurants shot up like mushrooms. But also a totally new way of building ecological houses, with healthy and sustainable materials developed.

In 1977 Amnesty International was given the Nobel Peace Prize. This association defends the human rights. Meanwhile, they have seven million members and supporters all over the world.

You could say that from the horrors of the Second World War, where over 70 million people died, a totally new consciousness was born. From this terrible collective mourning process arose a collective script transformation where values of peace, freedom, equality and respect for people and their environment were central.

In the sixties and seventies of the last century the term "spirituality" also get a new meaning. "Spirituality" is disconnected from religion and becomes "the search for the true self." Praying is replaced by meditating in re-connection with yourself. The "values" of the church as established order are questioned and the power of the church is crumbling. Spirituality becomes an individual experience.

We have described some strong post-war New Age movements and then we do not speak about the powerful movement that over-threw the Berlin Wall and communism in late eighties. But the roots of the new age are much deeper and the real inspirers are much older. I think of the philosopher, doctor, botanist, astrologer and occultist Paracelsus (1493-1541), which at the risk of his life, in his time already wrote down original ideas about medicine and psychology. Nostradamus (1503-1566) is most famous for his prophecies, but was also a progressive and modern thinking doc-tor. Another original thinking physician is Samuel Hahnemann (1755-1843). He is the inventor of homeopathy. Rudolf Steiner (1861-1925) and Ita Wegman (1876-1943) brought the homeopa-thic idea further in anthroposophic medicine. Meanwhile, Europe has several anthroposohist clinics, especially in Switzerland and Germany, where people who choose for a cure with homeopathy, can be treated successfully. Steiner is also on the basis of the so-called Steiner schools and biodynamic farming. Steiner schools offer a good alternative if you as a parent disagree with an educa-tion remaining stabbed in the integration pha-se wanting to pro-vide your New Age Children a happy school time. In terms of schools, the New Age offers truly multiple alternatives. I think of Célestin Freinet (1896-1966) and Maria Montessori (1870-1952), which are at the origin of Experience Oriented Education. And these schools are now in everyone's reach. Moreover, the thought of the New Education slips in the programs imposed by the government. They especially want to invite children to learn to think critically and for themselves. And that is progress.

Besides new Time Schools there are New Age nurseries where children get healthy food and wear bio Pampers. The staffs handle babies and toddlers more consciously.

New Age Mothers can give birth at home or in alter-native birth homes by the method of Frederick Leboyer (1918) and Michel Odent (1930) so babies are born without traumas for mother or child. You can read about this in Leboyer's and Odents books. Unfortunately, we see very little of this sublime wisdom applied in the clinics of the old world and in the doing of the old-time-gy-naecologists.

The Swiss Elisabeth Kübler-Ross (1926-2004) studied medicine against the mind of her father. With her hus-band Manny Ross she immigrated to New York, where she studied psychiatry. She felt the need to care for terminal patients and wrote many books about death, near-death experiences and OBEs. This the established order could not appreciate what ended up in an attack on her centre where everything was destroyed by a fire. She gave lectures about the transforming processes of mourning, which she as first described having successive stages: denial, anger, bargaining, depression and finally acceptance.

Other inspirers of the new world are Mahatma Gandhi (1869 - 1948) who realised in a peaceful and nonviolent way the independence of India (1947). And the Dalai Lama (1935), who brings messages of peace. He mana-ged to preserve the culture of Tibetan people, on the other side of the Himalayas in India. We also remember Nelson Mandela (1918 - 2013) as a preacher of nonviolence and peace. His dream was that blacks and whites could live peacefully next to each other in South Africa, and nowadays it happens. Martin Luther King (1929-1968) also cherished this dream, but he was kil-led for it. May it be comforting that in the beginning of the 21st century America with Barack Obama welcomed its first black president?

In the 80s and the 90th generation X trickled as young adults into society. This generation as a child has known economic crises. As graduates they struggled to find work. They were faced with companies that saved on labour. Gen X is fearful and conservative. At first sight, they are less socially engaged and more selfish and sticking more firmly to the old world. But meanwhile the new world grows and deepens and integrates and secretly we find many people belonging to gen X diligently helping in building the new era. It is more in-conspicuously and under the surface, but New Age spreads out on all sections of society.

I consider myself as fortunate, being able to live practical full-time in the New World and building on it, for example, as a guest lecture in Hanze University Groningen where I provide spiritual leadership courses. Or as a lecturer for the European Council giving presentations on script transformation when change happens for those who retire. Or when I give workshops for TransVormMensia. The new world I experience further when I buy organic food, when I have a consultation with the homeopath, when I am accompanying a constellation work, when I am in a coaching session, when I read a fascinating story on someone's blog, when I share information on Facebook, when I publish a book in own management, when I take part on an alternative book fair, when I attend children's theatre with my grand-children, when I visit an exhibition of a friend or when I participate in a spiritual festival, where I buy elves clothes. You can take part in shamanic sweat lodges or attend to workshop where you make your own shaman drum or Indians slippers. You can follow yoga class or meditate in an ashram. There are breathing workshops in Tantra and the awakening of the kundalini energy. You can let off steam in martial arts like Aikido and Tai Chi. You could have a weekend intuitive painting by the sea. You may become proficient in accompanying constellations, a course for life-coaching or craniosacral therapy. There are schools where you can learn for naturopath or herbalist or psychotherapist. You can study Ayurveda and homeopathy and herbal medicine and so much more. You just have to open up to and to step in.

We enjoy plenty the dawn of the New World, which is willing to be curative and constructive for everyone. In Flanders and the Netherlands her roots reach deep, so that hair crown begins to tower high. You just have to step in and to built on it, as the old world destroys itself and crumbles visibly.

It is perhaps appropriate to end with two texts that celebrate the coming of the Aquarian age. The first is a song from the musical Hair (1969), which was at the nativity scene of the New World and of which I enjoyed to the fullest in London as a New-time-Child. Beethoven's Ninth also sang about the coming of the new world. At the tail end you find my interpretation of this symphony in the form of a poem: "Ascension".

The Angel Aquarius

When the moon is in the Seventh House
And Jupiter aligns with Mars
Then peace will guide the planets
And love will steer the stars
This is the dawning of the Age of Aquarius
The Age of Aquarius
Aquarius! Aquarius!

Harmony and understanding
Sympathy and trust abounding
No more falsehoods or derisions
Golden living dreams of visions
Mystic crystal revelation
And the mind's true liberation
Aquarius! Aquarius!

When the moon is in the Seventh House
And Jupiter aligns with Mars
Then peace will guide the planets
And love will steer the stars
This is the dawning of the Age of Aquarius
The Age of Aquarius
Aquarius! Aquarius!

Ascension

I listen to the

Ninth symphony

By Beethoven

And I hear and feel and see

How the earth

Is born

In the fifth dimension

First she is at peace

Quietly she sleeps

In the divine kiss

Of a cold universe in expansion

In the sad third dimension

Where she lived

For ages and ages

She sails and swims

And softly she sings

And licks her wounds

In the Dark Age

Of the fish

The earth chooses

To be reborn

In Aquarius' age

Characterised

By real sisterhood

The turmoil comes

With the excitement

She is cheerfully

She is jokingly

The contractions begin

In slow regular spasms

She trembles and quivers and vibrates

Into a higher frequency

She's shaking towards the

Great galactic orgasm

She warms up

She gets up

Quietly awakens

Christ Love

In human souls

She hums

Seeing herself

Sparkling from afar

A glittering

Shining star

She sings harder

She dances faster

She waltzes merrily

With the moon

In orbit

Around the sun

She whistles

She whizzes

She   rocks

She wobbles

It was lovable

It was enjoyable

She was green

And gave life

And love

Melancholia

And sorrow

And suffering

Impatient Goodbyes

Looking back for a moment

And then she goes on

Dancing her way

To better times

She waddles and wobbles

And runs and jumps

As she's singing faster

And fluting harder

Suddenly

The pace accelerates

She rises upwards

She moans

She groans

No longer petrified

Supported by people

With wide awake awareness

She's mad, she's sad

Bravely she goes on

Resolute and firm

Growing pains overboard

No lasting harm

Pollution and global warming

Discontented grabbing

Selfishness and warfare

And nukes

She gave so much

And received so little in return

From the takers

Which became rich on her expense

All her generous gifts

Woodlands and plants

Minerals and ore

And oceans and pure water

Were taken

Were stolen

And made into private property

That is done

This comes to an end

She stands up

She spins

She rolls

She defrosts

She spirals upward

She runs with giant strides

In an impressive march

Urgently

In a haste

At a record rate

Homewards

In the realm of the gods

She wants to break through

She wants to break out

She wants to wake up

From the shackling matter

Which makes people asleep

She hops

She dances

She shines

Bubbles in her tummy

She dives

She throws herself

She gets light and lighter

She flies high and higher

She goes fast and faster

Sorrow becomes joy

Sadness becomes happiness

Pain becomes bliss

Her heart bursts

Her heart bangs

Her heart buzzes

Of excitement

She flies into a higher

Acceleration towards

The next dimension

Cheerful she goes on

Faster and faster

With great power

And yet soft

She walks

She hopes

She weeps

She turns

She runs

A true race

The contractions become more forceful

The emotions become more powerful

She is coming

We are coming

We come along

We are borne

Through our dear Mother Earth

We resonate

In a sea

Of zero point energy

We vibrate to a nicer regularity

We vibrate to a higher frequency

We finely come home

Lost sons and daughters

Are warmly welcomed

We see each other

We are each other

We recognize each other

We acknowledge each other

We embrace each other

It is a warm meeting

In true heart greeting

Love flows

Joy flows

We are Soul Brothers

From a past life

Rosicrucian and Cathar

Insiders who awaken

And perceive each other

Let us celebrate

Let us live in peace

Let us give bliss

This was the last incarnation

In the dark matter

Of the third dimension

It is done

It is cleared

We have succeeded

The angelic choirs descend

And join us again and forever

And out loud

We sing together

"Hymn to Joy

Joy, you beautiful divine spark

You daughter from Elysium

We enter, drunk with fire

Celestial being, your sanctuary

Your spells connect again,

Which divided the fashion sword

Beggars become princes

Where rest your friendly wings " (*)

Joy, joy, joy

The end of the Twilight of the Gods

Included in the arms of the one

Reunited with our divided essence

And our twin souls

The parade swells out

We are so many

Stars seeds and earthlings

Arcturians and indigo's

Light Beings and Crystal Children

Pleiadians and Sirians

And angels and guides

And we sing

"Gladly as his suns sail

Through the beauty

Of the heavenly plan

Brothers walk proudly your course,

Happily as a hero heading to victory.

Brothers, proudly walk your course

"Feel embraced, you millions

The whole world is enfold

In a divine kiss

Brothers! Above the starry sky

Must dwell a loving father

You fell down, you millions?

You expect the creator, world?

Find him above the starry sky

From above, the stars he should come " (*)

Beethoven already heard it

With its brightly hearing ear

His ninth symphony

Is about the ascension

From the Earth into the fifth dimension

All men become brothers

The creation is healed

Under the sign of Aquarius

The caretaker of the new age

For freedom and equality

All men become brothers

Under the guard of this constellation

(*) Free translation of Friedrich Schiller's text of the
Ninth Symphony of Beethoven

www.ingramcontent.com/pod-product-compliance
Lightning Source LLC
Chambersburg PA
CBHW020328290526
45785CB00007B/2957